D1496939

In the Land Where Time Began

Marion Prather Hays

Smyth & Helwys Publishing, Inc.
Macon, Georgia

ISBN 1-880837-35-8

In the Land Where Time Began
Marion Prather Hays

Copyright © 1993
Smyth & Helwys Publishing, Inc.

Library of Congress Cataloging-in-Publication Data

Hays, Marion Prather.
In the land where time began / Marion Prather Hays.
124 pp.   6x9" (15x23 cm.)
    ISBN 1-88-837-35-8   (alk. paper)
1. Bible. O.T.—Biography—Meditations. I. Title.
BS571.H34   1993
242'.5—dc20   93-32112
                                        CIP

Contents

Introduction vii

Chapter 1 The Tale of a Tower 1

Chapter 2 The Man from Across the River 7

Chapter 3 The Materialists 15

Chapter 4 Old Wells—and New 21

Chapter 5 The Unruly Twins 29

Chapter 6 The Dreamer 43

Chapter 7 The Ambitious Woman 57

Chapter 8 A Visit from an "In-Law" 65

Chapter 9 A Man of Valor 73

Chapter 10 A Woman Who Kept Faith with God 79

Chapter 11 A Pastoral Romance 85

Chapter 12 The Courageous Queen 95

Chapter 13 The Reluctant Missionary 109

For
Betty and Bill and Steele and Peggy

Introduction

I once heard a preacher say, "I don't need the Old Testament. I preach only Jesus Christ and Him Crucified." He thought of Jesus as having no past, as having sprung directly from Heaven in the manner of Minerva—"full-panoplied from the brow of Jove."

To me, part of the fascination of the Old Testament is that it contains the roots of Christianity. In its pages we can trace the emergence from paganism of a strain of people, their progression, oh so gradually, upward to the Prophets, and thence to the birth of Jesus with his divine philosophy of love. His roots were in Judaism; he drew on the scriptures for his knowledge, his wisdom, his strength, but he went beyond them. He said he did not come to destroy the past but to fulfill it. In him, it flowered and came to full fruition.

It has been truly said, "The past and future met in Jesus Christ." Then I think Jesus, instead of abandoning the trail so hardly and bravely won and followed by the Prophets and other heroes of the past, only led his disciples to climb to newer levels and wider dimensions. We are on that trail today, still climbing.

Chapter 1

The Tale of a Tower

Babel

One of the quaintest little stories in all literature (at least, that's what I think) is tucked away in the book of Genesis (11:1-9) and apparently well-nigh forgotten.

Perhaps the reason so little attention is paid to it is that it can have only the slightest basis in fact. But I like it because it does contain truth, which we all know is more important than fact—at least in the sense that it often tells us more.

This tale reminds me of the old *Fifty Famous Stories Retold*, which I enjoyed as a child, or of Uncle Remus, for it might be called *How Languages Were Born*. Actually, it is the story of the first skyscraper and what it led to.

After the flood—so runs the tale—when all the earth was of one language and one speech, a group of travelers, seeking suitable land to settle on, ventured west till they came to an attractive plain in the land of Shinar. (Shinar, according to Goodspeed, is an old name for a part, or all, of Babylonia.)

We are not told specifically who these people were, but since Noah had three sons, all equipped with wives, it is presumed that in the natural course of events the family would have increased rather quickly.

Our travelers decided they couldn't do better than make this lovely plain in Shinar their permanent home. They also decided to put up brick houses—an ambitious undertaking, as they had first to make the brick. The Hebrews of that early period were, of course, a nomadic people who lived in tents, and so one wonders if this detail isn't an anachronism. If Shakespeare could so overlook the realities when he wrote *Julius Caesar* as to provide Brutus with a striking clock, it need not surprise us if a more inexperienced and primitive writer should make a similar mistake. However it was, they did have to make do with tents while they all pitched in together to make the bricks. Apparently, they did have a recipe, for the bricks turned out well, and the men went happily to work building their homes.

While the work was still in its preliminary stages, someone came up with a large-scale idea. He said, "Let's not be satisfied with a little cluster of houses. Let's make a real city, with a tower in the center that will be tall enough to reach the heavens and will make us famous!"

Humankind's craving for fame, or even notoriety, began almost as soon as they did!

The suggestion was hailed enthusiastically.

"And there's another thing," someone else added. "To work together will hold us together, so that we won't get scattered abroad upon the face of the whole earth."

There wasn't a single dissenting voice. No chronic objector found fault because it wasn't *his* idea. No wet blanket protested that it was too big an undertaking, they couldn't possibly achieve anything so great, they should be satisfied with little aims, low goals. Their enthusiasm and harmony was an achievement in itself—not to say a miracle! And so they went happily ahead with their work.

But every story has to have conflict. No conflict, no plot. Since the writer had made it plain that all his characters were in agreement and things were going as smooth as butter, who was there to provide the conflict?

You'd never guess! (Unless, of course, you know already.) It was God!

Just how he learned that something unusual was going on, I don't know. Did Satan, perhaps, make mischief just for the fun of it? Anyway, God went down to see for himself, and there was the growing city, with a partly-built tower as its centerpiece, and the men of the community going about their work as cheerfully and busily as bees. It was a pleasant scene; exciting, even, if dedicated creativity appeals to you. But God didn't see it that way. He didn't like the project at all. He went back to his mountain top or sky home to think it over, and his reflections went like this: "This won't do! With a common tongue and a common purpose to unite them, they will be able to succeed at anything that occurs to them. I must prevent that. So let us go down and confuse their speech so that they won't be able to understand each other."

And that's what he did. He caused the people to speak in many different languages, so that they couldn't understand each other and couldn't communicate at all. The possibilities for comedy here are tremendous, if you visualize the efforts of a bricklayer and a carpenter, say, who were working efficiently together the day before, now unable to understand a single word the other is saying! Multiply this frustrated couple by dozens or hundreds, with the efforts to communicate getting noisier and angrier. I suspect Satan was laughing himself sick.

It was inevitable that the work should slow down and finally be abandoned altogether, and that the people, looking for more congenial situations, should scatter over the face of the earth. All that remains of a once-mighty effort is the name of the ill-starred city, Babel, a symbol of confusion and disappointed hopes.

The conflict had ended, and Humankind had lost. This is like the underlying philosophy of the Greek myths—that there was never-ending hostility between the gods and humans, and that life on earth was a perpetual warfare in which men pitted their puny strength against Olympus with no possibility of winning.

When this story was written down, many centuries after Noah's time, the scribes wisely preserved its ancient form, which is one reason it is a very valuable bit of lore. It gives us an insight into the simple minds and primitive religion of the people of a far-off day and at least a partial picture of the god they believed in. A very unfamiliar deity it is, too! Not much like the one we worship today. They thought he lived somewhere up high, in a definite place; if not in the sky, at least on a mountain top.

This God was not omniscient. When he wanted to see what men were up to, he had to go down where they were. When he wanted to check up on Sodom and Gomorrah, at a later time, he said to himself, "I will go down now and see if things are as bad as I hear they are!" (Gen 18:21).

After performing the miracle of confusing their speech, he went off home again, well-satisfied because he had defeated them and they could never be a threat to his power and greatness. His action was as petty, childish, and mean as any human being's on a bad day. In fact, he doesn't make nearly as good an impression on the reader as the people do! They didn't intend to defy him. Their ambition was natural and commendable. The instinct for self-preservation was involved: they were so few and the land so vast their fears of getting scattered and lost if they spread out were justified.

Their second purpose—to try to reach heaven while still on earth—that, too, was not bad, but good. Centuries later, Jesus told his hearers to do just that. "The Kingdom of Heaven is within you," he said. "Seek it and find it."

We can see that the truth that this story contains is much more important than any question of fact, for it shows us what a very ancient Semitic people thought about God and about life. Now what they thought about God was mistaken, but they had some ideas about life that are just as true now as then—and surprisingly timely for the twentieth century.

One of these ideas concerns the effectiveness of cooperation. That man in ancient Shinar knew what he was talking about when he made the suggestion that they should work together in order to stick together. He knew that a common purpose would bind them just as the slime bound the bricks that they made. As long as they were working together they spoke the same language, understood each other. If that unity had continued "nothing would have been restrained from them that they imagined to do." What a wonderful line! Those people who lived long before Moses, so long the date is unknown, knew that unity is constructive, disunity is destructive.

Now, we know much more about God, and we cannot accept the primitive interpretation of what happened at Babel. Let's give the incidents a different interpretation, based on our wider knowledge. Let's say that it was not God who interfered, but rather that jealousy and rivalry crept in, selfishness made itself felt, competition between different groups or families or clans destroyed the harmony. Perhaps there were disputes between labor and management. With so many factions pulling in different ways, inevitably the work stopped. To use some familiar metaphors, people no longer spoke the same language, or saw eye to eye. And so the splendid purpose fell through; the project was lost.

What a familiar story this is! A little fragment of life—now, as well as then. It reveals a truth about human nature that is the same yesterday and today—but not necessarily forever.

In 1945, after World War II was over, the world undertook a great building program. Representatives from fifty countries met in San Francisco and started work on a marvelous tower that was to be called the United Nations Organization. It was so new, so ambitious, so high-reaching, that some people didn't think it would get off the ground. "You can't prevent war," they said, "because you can't change human nature."

But there were more who had faith. These said, "We have never tried hard enough. We have never submerged our national jealously and distrust of each other to a common purpose. We *must* build this tower and see if it won't help us achieve our dream of a peaceful world."

And so the tower was started with high hopes. Unlike the ancient Semitic people, today's builders did not have a common language in the beginning, but modern science triumphed magnificently over that difficulty: translators using ear phones enable the delegates to hear the speeches and discussions in their own languages.

We have one great advantage the ancients did not have—we have God on our side, and we realize it. We know God is not an adversary or a competitor, but a partner. We believe God wants us to grow, develop, and learn all we can about the mysteries of the universe and that he tries constantly to reveal himself to us.

The doubters and cynics still say the United Nations is wasted effort, for we do not have world peace. But that we have started at all, have laid even two bricks together, is surpassingly wonderful. The subsidiary organizations it has fostered and supports, including UNICEF, the World Health Organization, and the United Nations Food and Agriculture Organization, are worth all they have cost, and the world would be poorer without them. When our spiritual development has caught up with our technical expertise, when we are as determined to submerge our national self-interest and partisanship as we were to conquer the handicap of the language barrier, when our determination to achieve a peaceful world is of paramount importance, then we will do it, and nothing can stop us. Human nature *can* change.

Maybe by the time the Tower is done and all nations have been brought into it (one hundred years from now? less?), Tennyson's dream will finally be realized, and we will have a Parliament of Man, a Federation of the World. Anything Humankind has the imagination to conceive can be realized with God's help, and then the old tower of confusion and defeat and disappointed hopes can be abandoned forever, and in its place will rise the Tower of Brotherhood.

Chapter 2

The Man from Across the River

Abraham

Once upon a time there lived in an ancient city named Ur, in the country of Chaldea, which lay in the beautiful and well-watered valley of the Euphrates River, a young man called Abram. He didn't know that long after his time people were going to look back to him and call him "the father of the Hebrews."

The Hebrews were only one group of ancient people known as Semites, or descendants of Noah's son, Shem. There were other Semitic nations, among them Arabians, Assyrians, and Phoenicians. A question that is still debated is whether Palestine originally belonged to Arabs or Jews. In the earliest known biblical times it was the Philistines' Land. Palestine, the name used today, is a form or corruption of the word Philistine.

How did *Abram* become the "father of the Hebrews"? He had forbears; he wasn't found under a cabbage. Then why wasn't the founder his father, Terah, or his brother, Haran? The answer is the story of how Abram found God.

When we become acquainted with him, he is living with his father and brother and their families in their hometown, Ur. He himself has just married a beautiful young girl named Sarai. In fact, she's so beautiful that a few years later (once in Egypt and once in Canaan) she attracted so much attention that Abram became afraid for his own life and twice did the unworthy thing of passing her off as his sister.

The people of Chaldea had two favorite deities—the sun and the moon god, whose name was Sin. We are told in Genesis 11:9

that following the flood, people were scattered over all the earth. Many generations came and went after the God-fearing Noah's time, before Abram was born to the line of Shem. Nothing is said about any of Noah's descendants knowing God. The feeble beginning of the true religion apparently died. Nothing indicates that Terah was any different from his compatriots of Ur. He is mentioned only as the father of Abram.

The Chaldeans are known to history as astronomers and students of the heavens. Henry Van Dyke made use of this fact when he made Artaban, hero of *The Other Wise Man*, a Chaldean, a believer in stars as messengers of truth to men.[1] Some of Artaban's friends were fire worshipers, followers of Zoroaster, a Persian priest who lived about a thousand years after the time of Abraham and urged worship of the sun god alone. Before his time, Chaldeans and other peoples of Mesopotamia worshiped many deities associated with the stars and planets.

If Abram hadn't had a good mind, and used it, he too would have lived and died knowing nothing better than to pour out his soul propitiating inanimate heavenly bodies, seeing and approving human sacrifice, thinking it was right for children to be bound to the altar in the temple at Ur and killed that the hungry gods might have blood to drink. For that was the horrible ritual prescribed by some of these heathen religions. If his son had been born there, he too might have followed the endless succession of hapless young victims.

But Abram was a thinker, and he found time in his busy days, or nights, to consider the nature of this religion, and I believe it was through the known—the heavens—that he reached the unknown. What is more likely than that he sat in the door of his tent at night and studied the starry sky? Like other Chaldeans, he must have been familiar with the stars and planets, their systems, and the regularity of their movements. Their courses were fixed, predictable for years ahead. He knew there was a marvelous harmony about them. How could they be so efficient up there, yet—if they were indeed gods—so erratic and capricious in their dealings with men? As he became more and more dissatisfied, wouldn't it be natural for him to come to the conclusions that there was a Master Mind that kept them in their course, a Power that regulated and ordered the heavens? That sun and moon and stars were just creatures, servants. Not gods at all.

France's great modern philosopher, Etienne Gilson, once said, "Belief in God has two sources, the human soul and the starry sky."[2]

I thought of Abraham. It seemed to me the two sources had met in him.

Of course, we know—and I'm sure the time came when Abraham knew—that that dissatisfaction and restlessness he was feeling was God's way of stirring him up and jarring him loose from the concepts that had possessed him from childhood. He is a perfect example of St. Augustine's affirmation, "Thou hast made us for Thyself, O God, and restless are souls until they rest in Thee."[3]

When he had made the great initial decision, Abram knew he couldn't stay there and remain free of the old futile worship. Certainly, he couldn't keep his family and servants free, and those were the days when a man was responsible for his household. Besides, this wonderful idea of his was a precious trust that he must transmit to his descendants. And so he left Chaldea and traveled west, like many another young man, until he came to Canaan. It was the Canaanites who gave him the title, *The Hebrew*, for the word means "the man from across the river." The river was the Euphrates.

That first obedient move was the most important step in Abram's whole life, and even though there were lapses and failures and backslidings in his life, God remained patient. His first bad mistake came early. It happened in Egypt, where they had gone because of famine in Canaan. As they drew near the border, Abram began to be afraid, or perhaps his fear had grown during the long days on the backs of their camels, riding across the desert. Those were days when kings had the bad habit of taking whatever they wanted, and Abraham had the feeling that the king of Egypt would want Sarai. He wasn't wrong, either! But Abraham, it is embarrassing to relate, was not so much afraid of what the Pharaoh would do with Sarai as of what he would do with him! And so he suggested a self-serving lie. "Say, I pray thee, thou art my sister, that it may be well with me . . ." (Gen 12:13).

There was no protest recorded from Sarai, but we needn't suppose she didn't make any, if only because her husband was thinking of his own safety instead of hers.

But Sarai went through with the pretense until the Pharaoh found out, as was probably inevitable. Furious at the deception, he sent for Abram and told him to take his false sister and his goods and get out. So they left, taking the fortune Abram had gained by this trick and the king's favor.

It is significant that there is no mention of an altar during this period of God speaking. It was a time of disobedience and dishonesty, of great fear, and of ill-gotten gains. When he got back to Canaan, a sadder and wiser man, he went directly to a place between Bethel and Ai where he had once built an altar and built another. It was a sign of repentance and hope that he could get back on the old basis with God.

God came to him there, forgave him, and repeated the promises.

As we look back on Abraham's life, we can see it as a pilgrimage, both literally and figuratively. As he traveled westward, he built altars to God. They marked both his geographical trail and his spiritual one; for as he moved onward, he was very gradually moving upward. We assume that he sacrificed animals on the altars, but if he had had children, it is conceivable he would have offered one of them, for it was not yet the *ritual* of his old religion that he objected to. It was the *deity*.

The story of his experiences, which was of course handed down from father to son, says that every now and then God appeared to Abram (they meant literally) and would make promises to him that had to do with his posterity (see Genesis 12 for one such appearance), and every time he had one of these experiences he built an altar unto the Lord.

But in spite of the promises, the years went by and no son was born to Sarai. It got to be something like a grim joke. When one part of his mind told him to believe God, the other part almost laughed. Once when he was walking at night, he thought God said, "Abram, can you count the stars? Well, neither will you be able to number your descendants" (Gen 15:5 and 17:7). Once

Abram said bitterly, "How are you going to do that? I'm still childless, and I'm growing old!"

Now Sarai wasn't dumb. She knew the great desire of Abram's life was to have a son. She knew how he brooded. No wife could fail to know. We know it was the custom for a man to have several wives, if he wanted them (and he usually did) and some concubines in addition. The fact that Abram had no other wife indicates real love between him and Sarai. So we can feel genuine sympathy and admiration for her at first, when she offered her husband her maid, Hagar. The situation was hopeless, she felt, and that action was the last resort.

Poor Sarai! If the stress in that family was bad before, it was nothing to what it became. For after producing a son, whom she called Ishmael, Hagar became impossible. She arrogantly flaunted her success and was openly contemptuous of the wife who hadn't fulfilled her destiny; while Sarai, I have no doubt, was bitterly jealous of Hagar.

It was at that time that Abram's name was changed to Abraham, which means "father of many nations," and God's promises to him he began to call a covenant. It was from that bargain that the Old Testament takes its name. He still persisted in his idea that Sarai was to be the mother of nations, a belief that was confirmed when God again appeared to him and said, "Sarai will have a son. Call him Isaac. My covenant will I establish with him—not Ishmael."

Finally, the incredible, the marvelous, thing happened! Sarai did, indeed, have a child, a fine little boy. Abraham's rejoicing was in proportion to his great longing and its delayed fulfillment (Gen 21:6). There were feasts and ceremonies when the baby was born, and more of the same when he was weaned.

And the boy grew. I believe he was a continuing delight to his parents. It was when Isaac was about twelve that Abraham had the greatest emotional and religious experience of his life, and learned the most important lesson he had yet learned about God, a lesson which was a turning point in religious history.

As we have seen, Abraham was not perfect, judged by the highest standards of morality, but the great moving purpose of his life was to be true to his trust, to keep his covenant with God. Out of this urgency was born his great idea—that he should seal this covenant with an offering. It must be a rare and precious gift, a real sacrifice, that would bind him and his descendants forever. Not just an animal, of which he had many, a common-place offering. It must be something better. And then, out of the experiences of his past, the awful thought was born, "It must be the dearest thing you have, nothing else is worthy—your son, your beloved son, Isaac."

I think Abraham's reaction to this idea was no different from what a father's today would be. It must have torn him like a searing flame. Undoubtedly, he wrestled with it for weeks; maybe months. I can see him debating with himself under the stars at night, and though the night would be cool, wiping perspiration from his brow. I can see him in the daytime watching Isaac, brooding over him with his heart in his eyes. I can see him as he felt himself being pushed nearer and nearer to the brink, saying in his soul, "This will be the last time I'll see him do that. . . ." Because he knew with a dreadful finality that he was going to do what he believed God wanted. God had given him his son, his delight for twelve years. For what purpose had he come if not for Abraham to return to God, thus sealing the covenant? This, to the poor distraught father, seemed the perfect bond.

He did not tell Sarai what he planned to do. He must have known her weight thrown against it would be too much for him to overcome. So early one morning, he and Isaac slipped out. Isaac saddled the ass. He knew they were going up on the slopes of Mount Moriah to make a sacrifice to the Lord. On the way he asked, "Father, we have everything but the lamb. What are you going to do about that?"

Abraham managed to answer, "God will provide himself a lamb, my son."

At what point did it begin to dawn on Isaac that he was to be the lamb? When the altar was built and everything ready, he looked at Abraham to see what was next and read the truth in his father's face. It must have been a fearful study in conflicting emotions—agony on account of the thing he was about to do, personal grief and sense of loss, thoughts of his old age without a son to lean upon—all this conflicting with zeal for his new religion, renunciation of self, and nobility of purpose.

What stayed his hand as it was raised ready to strike mercifully and quickly into the boy's heart? Some warning bell rang in his mind. Was it a mental picture of child sacrifice back in Ur? Was it the thought that back in Ur the people were offering their children to an unworthy god? *That he had left his home to get away from that ritual?* That since his God was different, he required a different worship?

All that, perhaps, was in his mind. And, too, a feeling that the intense love he had for his son was somehow connected, through the forces of life, with the Creator of the universe. For even as his hand was raised to plunge the knife into this child's heart, God spoke so commandingly to his spirit that he almost thought his ears had heard a voice. "Abraham, Abraham, lay not thy hand upon the child!" Whenever he told that story afterward (and I imagine Isaac asked for it many times), he always said that *God spoke to him and called him by name.*

And so Abraham broke from the last remnants of the old pagan ritual and came to believe in a God who abhorred human sacrifice. This belief he passed on to his son Isaac, and his grandson, Jacob. That was one of the great milestones in humanity's struggle to understand God and his will for humanity, for it is the first recorded instance in which an animal was substituted for a child, and the deity was satisfied.

Yet Abraham's posterity, because of the pagan influence of the tribes they lived among, did not remain entirely free. They sometimes practiced child sacrifice, infanticide by exposure (putting them out in the woods or fields to die), or selling them into slavery. But it was always at a minimum among the Hebrews, even while practiced generally and openly by the Greeks and Romans.

The attitude of the Greeks toward parenthood was one of cold-blooded selfishness. Four centuries before Christ, Plato described a perfect city state—population 5040, the level to be maintained by infanticide, abortion, and regulation of unions. In Athens the practice was to bring up one child or none.

Rome, throughout her history, retained child exposure as one of the most common of all social customs, although from the time of Romulus she made an effort to eliminate it. The first Roman laws were attributed to Romulus. One of these was that no healthy male child could be exposed, and that each family must keep one female. I suppose someone had a belated awareness that females played some small part in the perpetuation of the race! The law decreed that all children must live till they were three years old, but at that age extra females and cripples or unhealthy babies of either sex could be exposed if five relatives approved. That was the first recorded decree against unlimited exposure, but the Romans never took it seriously. Augustus instituted tax exemption for each child reared, but still the inhuman practice continued, a proof that love and compassion cannot be successfully created by legislation. For the thing that finally put an end to this cruel custom was the Christian religion, and the acceptance of God as a Father of infinite compassion was due to the life and teaching of one of Abraham's descendants.

This is the story of how Abraham became the father of the Hebrews, the friend of God, the keeper of the covenant.

Notes

1(New York: Harper, 1899).
2*The Christian Philosophy of Saint Augustine*, trans. L. E. M. Lynch (New York: Random House, 1960)
3*Confessions of St. Augustine* (New York: Pocket Books, 1952).

Chapter 3

The Materialists

Mr. and Mrs. Lot

Like most people, Abraham had more than one problem complicating his life. In addition to the friction in his own home, there was the relationship with his nephew, Lot, and his niece by marriage, Lot's wife.

Lot had elected to leave Ur with the rest of the family, so we can assume the relationship to have been close and the members congenial. Terah, Abraham's father, had died and been buried in Haran, where they had sojourned for awhile, and Lot's father had died before they had moved out of Ur; but Abraham, Lot, their wives, and dependents had remained together. A famine in Canaan drove them to Egypt, and by the time they returned to Canaan, the Lots had two daughters.

Mrs. Lot's failure to produce sons was no doubt disappointing, but all things being relative, the fact that she had done so much better than Aunt Sarai must have made her pretty well satisfied with herself. Anyone with half an eye could see that Aunt Sarai was out of favor with the God Jehovah that Uncle Abraham set such store by. Uncle Abraham was already old, and Mrs. Lot may have felt he was a trifle childish, especially in his insistence on building altars everywhere and his emphasis on worship.

This is only a guess, but she may have been the key to the separation of Lot from the uncle who had been foster father to him and made him rich in this world's goods. Something came between them. The story just says the herdsmen of the two men quarreled, but I strongly suspect that was only an excuse and there was more to the rift than that. Quarreling servants could have been dealt with pretty summarily. What I would like to know is how Mrs. Lot and Aunt Sarai got along.

When they arrived in Canaan the second time, Uncle Abraham did a characteristic thing. He said, "You choose the piece of land you want, and I will go in the opposite direction."

If Lot had made an unselfish choice—if he had said, "You choose first, Uncle Abe. You've always been good to me, made me rich. I'd rather you had first choice"—the whole course of his life might have been different. We learn something fundamental about Lot at this point: he was neither unselfish nor grateful. He looked over the land, saw the richness of the Jordan valley. He might have thought, "I'll leave that for Uncle Abe." But he did not. "Lot chose him all the plain of Jordan. And Lot journeyed east, and they separated themselves, the one from the other" (Gen 13:11).

"Lot chose him. . . ." That has a callous ring to it that I believe was intentional. That action was merely the first in a series of mistakes, but important because it was the turning point. When he separated himself from his uncle, it was from the best influence in his life. Abraham, like the grand old man he was, took what was left and moved off to the west, while Lot "pitched his tent toward Sodom." By this choice, he put himself and his family, who were not well-grounded in the new religion, in the way of temptation. There is no suggestion that he ever built an altar to Jehovah or carried on the family worship. There is no mention of periods of meditation when God could have spoken to Lot as he did to Abraham. If there was any attempt to impress on their daughters the high standard of personal purity and righteousness consonant with the worship of Jehovah, it did not get into the record. My belief is Mrs. Lot was too busy running after the Baal-worshiping society of Sodom. So completely unfaithful were they to the religion Abraham had instituted at the time the family left Ur that when the city would have been spared for ten righteous people, they were not to be found. Although there were at least six in Lot's own family, the older daughters now being married, and hoards of servants, Lot's influence had been so negligible that the number could not be met.

At this point, the story becomes very dramatic in a quaint and primitive way, for the details are based on old concepts that the Hebrews themselves abandoned as time went on. The Lord said, "I will go down now and see for myself what is going on in

Sodom and Gomorrah, for I fear from the cries that have come to my ears that their sins are grievous."

The idea that God lived on a mountain and would have to come down where men were in order to know what was going on was held until the children of Israel, under Joshua, entered Canaan. The conversation with Abraham that followed, about sparing the city, was thought to be a face-to-face exchange and was in the pattern of Oriental bargaining still followed to this very day. According to the story, it was Abraham who pointed out to God the injustice of destroying the righteous with the guilty. It was Abraham who had compassion for the people, stupid and sinful as they were, and who pled with an indignant God. After the bargaining had ended, "The Lord went his way," as a human being would have done.

The crudity of these concepts proclaims their great age. In comparison with those of the New Testament, they are like pieces of ancient pottery dug up by an archaeologist juxtaposed to a set of French Havilland china; but they interest us exceedingly and are of great value because they were once held to be true and because they are the foundation of our present beliefs.

As the story mounts to a climax, it becomes even more fantastic. Such details as Mrs. Lot's gruesome end never seem to happen nowadays. Also, the arrival of plain-clothes angels to stage-manage in person the destruction of Sodom adds to the bizarre scene. Lot didn't seem to see anything remarkable about that, but then I never regarded Lot's perceptiveness as being superior! In every way, except as a money-maker, he seems to me just barely average.

The difference in the attitudes of Lot and his uncle to the fate of Sodom is revealing. To Lot, it was home. He lived there, had friends and in-laws. Yet he was concerned only for himself and his immediate family. Abraham had chosen to live in the hills, and was not even acquainted with people in the two cities, but he was concerned for them and did what he could to save them. This has been called the first case of intercessory prayer.

The angels had to lead Lot and his family out by force. Then they warned them, "Flee to the mountains! Save yourselves!"

Lot looked at the mountains and shuddered. The materialistic life he had been leading had such a hold he couldn't imagine living any other way. He pointed out a small city and begged to go there. "That my soul may live!" was his stupid entreaty. It wasn't big and sinful—just little and sinful.

The angel answered, "Well, hurry! We can't start till you're out of the way."

The destruction came, fire and brimstone from the skies. They could hear the crackle of flames, the screams of victims.

"Do not look back!" the angels cautioned.

Dr. Clovis Chappell once pointed out that only someone who was ignorant of human nature would give that command and expect it to be obeyed. Not God, who created human beings and thoroughly knew their nature and their weaknesses. A woman who was not personally involved and to whom the holocaust was only a spectacle would have felt an irresistible urge to turn and look, but this woman was tragically and horribly concerned. She must see if their house, hers and Lot's, was really going to catch a fire. Yes! There it went! The roof gave way. The neighbors' houses, too. The whole block—a sheet of flame!

If God had wanted to punish her severely it would surely have been for some of the things she did not do—for her empty, purposeless life; for the opportunities she did not use; for the women she did not influence—not because she showed more curiosity than was advisable at that moment.

I don't believe God would have turned her into salt, anyway. What could have been more inappropriate? Salt has a saving quality. It's a blessing and a boon to mankind, while Mrs. Lot was a perfect cipher. Her life counted for nothing in her community.

In my youth I heard more than one stirring sermon preached by evangelists on the text, "But Lot pitched his tent toward Sodom." It's a wonderful springboard for the old-fashioned emotion-stirring sermon. Symbolically, it was the beginning of Lot's spiritual decay. But literally in what way, if at all, is this applicable to us? Should we stay away from a big sinful city? If so, what is your excuse—or mine—for living in Washington? or New York? or any metropolis? People in small towns and rural areas are apt to think there is something sinful about size. I've been asked at my home city of Little Rock if the people in Washington aren't cold and worldly, and the churches empty. I was able to tell them I had never met more sincere and dedicated Christians anywhere! If our ideals are not strong enough to stand the temptations of a city, neither will they stand those of a town.

The important thing was not where the Lots lived, but how they lived. Their aims were selfish, their ambitions unworthy, their ideals low.

If you work in an office among irreverent and irreligious people, should you get out—or be a missionary? Abraham could have settled in Sodom and not been contaminated. Every situation would have been an opportunity for good.

Jesus deliberately went where sinners were, and he gave us our directive, "Hate the sin, but love the sinner," and feel a responsibility for him.

Lot may have rationalized, "No one knows or cares what I do. It can't possibly matter. I can go to church or stay at home. I can relax, take it easy." And Mrs.Lot may have defended herself with the old alibi, "What can I do, one woman in a big city? I have no influence."

A young woman came to Washington during World War I. She was alone, and away from home, but she had a high opinion of the importance of one woman. She said to herself, "I must do something with my time besides just feed and clothe myself. What shall it be? I could teach a Sunday School class of business girls."

But she found there was no such class in her church. Mrs. Lot would have said, "Well, that lets me out. No one could expect me to teach a class if there isn't any."

But Jessie Burrall organized a class, and under her dynamic leadership it attracted literally hundreds of young women who had come to Washington to work in offices and who had not established a church home. She had a talent for organization, but even more importantly she had enthusiasm and dedication, and the class she started with a handful of girls grew to over a thousand. It outgrew the room assigned to it in the church, so permission was obtained to meet in a theatre across the street, the Rialto, which was closed on Sundays. Passers-by would stare to see hundreds of young women pouring out of the theatre at eleven o'clock on Sunday morning!

Burrall class is still an active force for good and a living memorial to Jessie Burrall, who lived in a big city in which there were doubtless plenty of sinners; but she established her altar, and the light of its fire warmed and inspired many a girl who might have gone the way of Mr. and Mrs. Lot.

Perhaps Mrs. Lot did not have the talent or the personality that Jessie Burrall did, for the latter was exceptional, but she had one asset of great importance. She had a home, probably an attractive one, for her husband was a rich man. She had two young daughters who had at least the potential for making that home a cheerful and inviting place. If it had also been one where God was honored, the neighborhood would have been a different place.

In some reading I came across a phrase I like—"the creative witness of a Christian home." For those of us who are neither preachers nor evangelists but home-makers, I think the most effective witnessing we can do is to maintain such a home. No preaching or arguing is necessary. Silently, the radiance speaks for itself. And we can safely leave to God the blessing of those who come within the orbit of its influence. If we provide the setting and the opportunity, God doesn't need to be told what to do with it!

Chapter 4

Old Wells—and New

Isaac, A Man of Peace

Did you ever wonder what kind of a man Isaac turned out to be? The young boy who was so obedient and compliant he was nearly sacrificed without a protest or a struggle to his father's mistaken idea of God's will?

Well, as far as we can judge by the few facts recorded, in themselves a kind of negative testimony, he became a gentle, peaceable undemanding man. Certainly he accepted his father's decision that he should refrain from any romantic involvement with the young women of Canaan, with the result that he was still a bachelor at forty (Gen 25:20). And it was Abraham, concerned about keeping his covenant with Jehovah, but realizing the line would die out if Isaac had no son, who found a solution: he would send back to Mesopotamia, "to my country and to my kindred," (he thought) and solicit a wife among Isaac's cousins. Abraham's older brother, Haran, had died long ago in Ur, but he had a younger brother, Nahor, who must have some descendants, even if he, too, was dead. Without knowing anything about these connections, or whether, like the rest of Ur, they worshiped the sun and moon, he felt, like many another man, that anyone related to himself would be preferable to those who were not!

So he sent a confidential servant on this mission. It would be interesting to know why he did not let Isaac go himself, since he was the one most nearly concerned. Could he have feared that Isaac would not return but would decide to settle down in Mesopotamia? At any rate, it was a shrewd move, considering what we learn later about the girl's brother, Laban, a smooth trader who might well have prevailed on Isaac to remain permanently with his wife's family.

So Abraham's steward (who is never named) set out with ten camels and "jewels of silver and gold, and raiment," evidence of the wealth and status of his master. He arrived at evening at the town of Padonaram, where Nahor lived, and stationed himself at the well on the outskirts of town, knowing the village maidens would soon be coming to fill their pitchers, for this was a task traditionally assigned to the women. His careful plans included the response he hoped to get from the girl who would be his first choice. It would be a sort of test—when he respectfully asked for a drink, he hoped she would be courteous and obliging and would offer to water his camels also.

Pretty soon, here they came, a bevy of girls, laughing and chattering, for the well was the focal point of social life. His attention centered upon one, whom he considered the most attractive, and to his great satisfaction the conversation went along the lines he had imagined. In fact, even further, for the damsel, perhaps impressed by his manner, said, "Drink, my lord," and after he had been satisfied, she emptied her pitcher into the trough until the camels had had enough.

Things couldn't have been more pleasing, the steward thought, when he learned that the maiden, whose name was Rebekah, was the granddaughter of Nahor, Abraham's brother, and that there would be room for him and his camels at her father's house. It could hardly be otherwise when they heard his story and saw the golden earring and two bracelets of gold he had already given Rebekah at the well. Bethuel, her father, and her brother, Laban, without the slightest hesitation bestowed their daughter and sister upon the unknown but wealthy suitor and received their own lavish gifts, for Abraham had sent plenty. Rebekah's mother did ask the next day, "What's the rush? Stay at least ten days with us"; but the emissary, true to his trust, said, "No, I must get back." They went through the formality of asking Rebekah if she wanted to go, and she said yes. And so the caravan departed.

Some days later, Isaac went out to meditate in the field at eventide, and he lifted up his eyes and behold, the camels were coming! The meeting was a happy one. The steward's mission had been successfully accomplished.

An illustrator who was famous when I was young, W. L. Taylor, painted for the *Ladies' Home Journal* a series of portraits of Bible women as he envisioned them. There was one of Rebekah at the well, a lovely dark-haired girl in flowing robes, with a large pitcher resting on her shoulder. Her eyes were clear and untroubled, her brow serene, her mien dignified. The damsel was, indeed, very fair to look upon, the steward thought.

In all probability, however, the reality was somewhat different, for the Rebekahs among the ancient Hebrews were usually the family drudges, going to the well many times a day and returning with a heavy crock of water. They must have gotten very tired and very hot and felt very unromantic about the whole business. Maybe that is why Rebekah agreed so readily to go to Canaan with Abraham's servant! But knowing girls, I imagine they would have found some pleasures in even this monotonous life, and perhaps the evening gossip at the well was one of those.

At any rate, a commentator observed, "There would have been no Rebekah in Art if there had been no Rebekah at the Well."

Rebekah didn't know it then, but the wells of Canaan were to play an important part in her married life.

Eventually, as it must to all men, death came to Abraham. He was old and full of years and was buried beside Sarah at Hebron.

Now Isaac was the Patriarch. He was a different type altogether from his father. If I had to name one tangible thing that seems to me typical of Abraham's life, I would say the altar. Everywhere he paused in his travels, no matter how briefly, he set up an altar to the Lord. I imagine it was just a simple erection of stones, but it symbolized his dependence on God and his daily association with him.

In the case of Isaac, the thing that comes to my mind is a well. Not bad for second place, for next to the altar the well was the most important thing in life. Physical existence in that desert land was dependent upon it.

Isaac was not, however, in the beginning much of a digger. It was Abraham, moving about Canaan with his flocks and herds, who had dug the wells. After his death, his son ran into trouble. The flocks and herds now belonged to him, and as he moved about Canaan in his father's footsteps, expecting to reclaim and use his father's old wells, he found it impossible without a fight with the Philistines, who were now camping there (Gen 26:14). In some cases, they were moved by simple envy of the Hebrew's wealth and sometimes vented their spite by filling up the wells with rocks and dirt—a strange revenge when water was such a precious commodity!

The first time this happened, Isaac called off his tribesmen and moved on to another place, Gerar, where he knew his father had dug a well. But it, too, had been ruined. As soon as his servants had cleaned it out—and what a job!—the herdsmen of Gerar came and said, "The well is ours. Get out!"

Again, Isaac moved on, this time to Sitnah, where the same thing happened. Again, it was fight or withdraw. Again, he moved on. I have little doubt his herdsmen were itching to fight it out, but Isaac could not deny his own nature. He was a gentle person, and he hated violence. Each time he moved, he was optimistic that at the next place they would be more fortunate. As hard as the job of cleaning out a well was, it was easier and surer than to sink a new shaft. Where water had once been found, it would be again. Also, there was a sentimental reason—they were his father's wells.

Isaac is not the only person to sentimentalize over water from a certain source. You will remember that once when he was sick, David had a feverish longing for a cup of water from a certain well at Bethlehem, and women went to great trouble to get it for him. One of our old folk songs is about the old oaken bucket that hung in the well. To James Whitcomb Riley, the water that came from that well in his boyhood had never been equaled for flavor!

Isaac probably convinced himself that his reluctance either to make a stand against hostile men, or to take on the difficult task of locating and opening up a new source of water, was a virtue. But, fortunately, he got discouraged finally! So discouraged that he turned to God for guidance. His self-confidence had evaporated. This was a very serious business, and he didn't know what to do! But man's extremity has always been God's opportunity, and when Isaac was ready to listen, God was ready to comfort him with a sense of his presence and support, just as he used to do with his father. Isaac drew strength also from that encounter, and the next day, or soon after, he gave orders to test for a new well. The servants dug, and they found water!

That must have been a wonderful day and a very satisfying experience, far surpassing in depth and intensity the pleasure of drinking again from his father's old well. For the first time, Isaac knew the deep creative joy of providing a new source of refreshment for thirsty humanity, of bringing life to an arid spot where there had been none before. He, the gentle, rather ineffectual, man had created something of his own. It's not hard to imagine the rejoicing in Isaac's household that day.

Walter Russell Bowie in *Great Men of the Bible* has described an interesting conversation he once had with a stranger on a train, "a pleasant gentlemen, who turned out to be a minister on his way to a convention of his church." Bowie continued: "He told me in the conversation of some of the matters most interesting to him which were to arise, and the one he described with most enthusiasm was the program of the 'fundamentalists.' The convention was to see the issue fought between the men of modern scholarship, who represented the liberty of religious inquiry, and those who were determined to lay down certain fixed unalterable definitions which they called the fundamentals, beyond which no one should be allowed to range without being proclaimed a heretic. The minister on the train was an ardent supporter of the fundamentalists, and he told me how he had preached the previous Sunday on the text, 'And Isaac digged again the wells of water, which they had digged in the days of Abraham his father; for the Philistines had stopped them after the death of Abraham: and he called their names after the names by which his father had called them' (Gen 26:18). He made it a plea for conservatism that should be absolute. As Isaac drank from his father's wells, so the church ought to drink from the words of teachers of yesterday, and never dare sink its shafts of thought anywhere beyond their borders.

"He seemed surprised when I asked him if it had occurred to him that Isaac, whose act he took as his pattern, was after all a second-rate figure in the history of Israel, while Abraham, who had not dug again *his* father's wells but had dug new ones, was the creator of that great religious experience that all the rest of the Old Testament goes on to expand."

I couldn't help feeling a bit sorry for the fundamentalist—he must have felt so silly! He had overlooked such an obvious truth. And even Isaac was a contradiction to the preacher's argument, for when he was pushed hard enough by circumstances, he went forward.

Perhaps he lacked Abraham's mystical nature. He didn't build so many altars, but his father's God was very real to him. And God's directive was *not* to make a stand and fight for old wells. Neither was it to do nothing except just keep moving on. God would never give advice like that. What he did tell Isaac was to take a *new and positive action*—to leave the old and undertake the new.

Tradition and sentiment are very strong, but they can be overcome. Conservatism has its place, and its best function is to follow new gains—for a time! But not for too long a time. That's the mistake the ultra-conservative mind so often makes: every time it accepts, no matter how regretfully, anything new, it proceeds to solidify the new position so that it, in its turn, will be final. If the world had been satisfied with old wells, we wouldn't have the joy of modern plumbing, and if it had never accepted new truth, we would never have believed the teachings of Jesus. Rigidity of mind results in a hardening of the spiritual arteries and is the greatest hindrance to the pursuit of truth.

We must not dismiss Isaac's gentleness and love of peace as a weakness, for the day came when it proved its power. In fact he had another triumph, much greater than that of producing a well of his own, important as that was. One day he had a surprise visit from Abimelech, the chieftain who lived near Gerar and whose tribesmen had driven off Isaac's. He brought with him the head of his army and another man, and he came to make peace and offer friendship. Isaac was surprised to the point of bewilderment at first, but with a fine frankness Abimelech expressed his admiration for Isaac because of his forbearance and patience, his lack of arrogance and false pride.

That was a very surprising attitude on the part of a Philistine, and as great a tribute to him as to Isaac. But why should we be surprised? Surely we don't think God speaks only to us and our friends and through our channels alone; that he has nothing to say to—well, to Russians, for instance. "My Father works, and I work," Jesus said, and I think he meant they work independently of us.

Isaac's pacifism got results that belligerence would never have done. His conduct, I believe, was what Jesus meant by "turn the other cheek." Not a literal and limited interpretation, as useless as it is humiliating. He meant to be great enough to contain anger, to swallow small irritations, and to be compassionate enough about big ones to pity the poverty of spirit that your enemy or opponent may reveal. Many encounters, Jesus knew, would end just like this one, in peace and good will instead of friction, if one would "turn the other cheek."

Miss Jessie Burrall once related an experience that is a perfect example of the power of a soft answer. She was on a street car in Washington, standing, because it was crowded. When the car took on more passengers, one was a man, whose elbow accidentally struck her. He was already mad when he got on, and he continued to scowl.

She looked pleasantly back at him and said, "Excuse me." He made no answer.

Two people who saw and heard looked at her as if they were thinking, "Well, you dumbbell! Don't you know when you've been hit?"

Finally, the man looked at her out of the corner of his eye, then turned and muttered, "I beg your pardon. My fault."

"When he got off," Miss Burrall said, "he had relaxed visibly. The frown was gone. The people he met that evening were safer. And it cost me so little."

Isaac was one of the peacemakers of history. He earned a wonderful epitaph, "Blessed are the peacemakers, for they shall be called the children of God."

Chapter 5

The Unruly Twins

Esau and Jacob

Part I

Isaac and Rebekah are generally thought of, I believe, as a couple who fell in love at first sight, married, and lived happily ever after. She had been presented as a bride to a husband she had never met, a situation that crops up from time to time in song and story, because it is often regarded as romantic, and the happy outcome—love after marriage—is inevitable.

But in this case, at least, the reality differs somewhat from the legend. The fact is they were singularly ill-matched. While Isaac did indeed feel attracted at once to Rebekah's pleasing face and figure, nothing is recorded about how Rebekah felt about Isaac. There is no evidence that she ever loved him, either at first sight or hindsight!

Unfortunately, Rebekah did not wear well. As she grew older she revealed a nature that was calculating, determined, even ruthless. Isaac, on the other hand, was gentle, peaceable, forbearing, and trusting.

They had only two children, a small family for those times, but those two made up in activity for what they lacked in numbers, for they were a handful from birth. Or even before birth, for they surprised everyone, including the midwife, by arriving together; that is, on the same occasion. Esau was actually born first.

The two boys, instead of sharing an affinity as twins often do, were as different as their parents. Jacob, the younger, either inherited his mother's deviousness or followed her example. In any case, their temperaments were congenial, so that Jacob was very much the child of his mother and became her favorite son.

There is not a chance that Esau failed to perceive this favoritism, for children are preternaturally sensitive to such distinctions. He spent a good deal of time out of doors in the woods and fields, away from the family tents where he was spared the sight of his mother petting and spoiling his brother. He became a skillful hunter, easily able to bring down a deer with his bow and arrow. Isaac dearly loved venison, and this taste made a bond between him and Esau, which helped compensate the older boy for the mother's love he never received. So father and son drew close together for companionship and consolation, with the result that the family became a house divided.

Rebekah, strange, unnatural mother that she was, viewed with displeasure the intimacy of her husband and his heir. She coveted for her favorite the birthright that in the normal course of events would go to Esau, and she began early to hatch schemes to obtain it for Jacob. For Isaac to have a favorite son, too, and that son the one she wanted to defraud, made her conniving more difficult.

The Hebrew birthright, which by tradition descended to the eldest son, was a two-fold inheritance. It carried a spiritual blessing as well as the lion's share of the father's wealth. Rebekah cared nothing, I'm afraid, for the spiritual blessing, that was based on the covenant Abraham made with Jehovah, but she cared a great deal about the material wealth which would come with it. That wealth, she was determined, must be Jacob's.

Unconcerned for her husband's failing health, she made her plans to deceive him and to circumvent both his will and Jewish tradition. A fault in Esau himself played into her hands. In a weak moment, when he had come in from the fields hungry and tired and found Jacob about to eat a bowl of freshly-made pottage, he wanted it so badly that when Jacob said, "I'll trade it for your birthright," Esau answered, "Done!"

One can put several constructions on this idiotic deal. So much condemnation has been heaped on Esau that he is often regarded as a glutton, a sensualist, a man who lived for the moment, who exchanged lasting value for tinsel; the man who put the expression "a mess of pottage"—to give up a worthy goal for an immediate temporary satisfaction—in the language. In short, a mess!

I want to suggest that such harsh blame for one mistake is not justified. I can think of some reasons for Esau's foolish action that seem to me probable. Perhaps he thought it was impossible for Jacob to collect on such a bargain, just as Jacob could not change the fact of Esau's prior birth. Or that it was not a bona fide trade because Jacob could not be serious. Admittedly, these reasons are not admirable, but they do remove from Esau the stain of indifference to the birthright.

Maybe Jacob *wasn't* serious. But when Rebekah heard about it, that put a different complexion on the deal. She knew, now, how she was going to achieve her purpose!

The day came when Isaac, realizing that he was failing fast, told Esau the time had arrived when he was to receive his birthright. First, like a ritual feast, he would have some of the delicious venison he loved, and so Esau must go to the woods and kill and then prepare a young deer.

That was also the day Rebekah had been waiting for. She summoned Jacob and revealed her plan for outwitting her husband and her other son. He was to get in first with some goat stew from their own flocks, and since Isaac was very feeble and nearly blind, he would be easily deceived.

Jacob was perfectly willing but raised one objection. "He may be suspicious. What if he even wants to feel my hands or arms? My brother's a hairy man, and I'm smooth. He could tell the difference in a moment."

"Well, then, I'll put some of the goat skin on you. He can feel that!"

She was like Lady Macbeth, who ruthlessly pushed her husband to do a vile deed: "But screw your courage to the sticking place, and we'll not fail."

The plan was carried out. But Isaac wasn't quite so easy to fool as Rebekah had thought. He was nearly blind, but he had good ears! And he was suspicious. First, of Jacob's voice. Jacob had said only two words, "My father . . . " when Isaac asked, "Who are you?"

"I am Esau, thy first born. I have brought you your venison. Sit up and eat, so you can bless me," answered Jacob.

But Isaac wasn't so stupid, either. "How have you done this so quickly?" he demanded.

Jacob thought fast. "Uh, God was with me. He brought the deer to me."

Still suspicious, showing how little he trusted his younger son, Isaac demanded, "Come near. I want to feel you."

Jacob, thankful for his mother's sharp wits, stretched out his arms.

Faced with this evidence but not really satisfied, the old man said, "The voice is Jacob's voice, but the hands are the hands of Esau."

And so he blessed him.

"God give thee of the dew of heaven, and the fatness of the earth, and plenty of corn and wine. Let people serve thee and nations bow down to thee. Cursed be every one that curseth thee, and blessed be he that blesseth thee."

A very comprehensive endowment! If Isaac had had it in his power to bestow such largesse, Jacob would have had no problems for the rest of his life. To get it, he had lied three times and had acted the part of a scoundrel.

He had hardly gone—perhaps to report the success of his deception to his mother—when Esau came in with the venison that he had prepared. It was the real thing, not goat stew. The scene that followed is one of the most poignant in the Old Testament. Isaac, trembling with age and emotion, confessed he had been deceived, he had blessed the wrong son, and recognizing the irrevocability of the act, exclaimed, "Aye, and he shall be blest."

Esau, who did value the birthright, however foolishly he had seemed to disregard it, cried with an exceedingly great and bitter cry, *"Hast thou but one blessing?* Bless me, even me also, O my Father!"

But according to the sad custom of the time, there was no other blessing!

Esau's reaction was anger against his brother that shook him to his foundations. He announced bluntly that he would hold off only until his father had been buried and mourned (not that he was yet dead, but the event did seem to be imminent), and then he was going to see to it personally that his brother followed his father out of this world without any loss of time.

Now at last the ugly traits that had made Rebekah a failure as a wife and mother caught up with her. She had set in motion a train of events she could not control and which she must have regretted bitterly. She knew Esau was serious, and she was terrified for the safety of the only person she loved, so she was obliged to send him away. "Get ready quickly, my son, and flee to my brother Laban in Haran, and tarry with him a few days until thy brother's fury shall turn away from thee and he forgets what you did to him. When it is safe, I will send for you."

And so by her own acts, she lost both her sons.

To arrange this, however, she had to have Isaac's consent and cooperation. Like all women of the time, she had to use the regular channels of authority, so she had to appeal to the husband she had mocked and deceived for permission to equip Jacob for his journey. Once more she deceived poor old Isaac! It was time Jacob married, she said, and she simply couldn't bear it if he followed his brother's example and married Hittite girls.

"I have been weary of my life ever since Esau married those daughters of Heth. If Jacob should do that, what good would my life be to me?"

She knew Isaac had deplored the alliance with Philistine families, but Esau was forty years old when he married, and there was no one else. What was he to do? If Isaac had known as much about his brother-in-law, Laban, as Jacob was to learn, he might have felt that Esau could have done worse! As he did not, and as he felt the same way about relatives as his father Abraham had felt before him, he called Jacob to him and charged him, "Thou shalt not take a wife of the daughters of Canaan. Go to Padanaram, to the house of your grandfather, and there choose a wife from among the daughters of your Uncle Laban. And may God Almighty bless thee."

And Jacob went out from his home and traveled toward Haran.

He was gone twenty years.

Part II

From this point the story becomes Jacob's, for we follow his fortunes as he goes back to Haran to seek out his Uncle Laban and to find a bride among his cousins.

At sunset of the first day, he picked out a pleasant spot to spend the night. He had, of course, brought food and water, and as he was tired from his long trek he soon made his preparations to go to bed. These were simple—he put a few stones together to support his head, and then lay down and went to sleep. As he slept, he dreamed. He saw a ladder that reached from earth to heaven, and moving up and down upon it were angels of God. As he gazed, he saw the Lord at the top, and he said to Jacob, "I am the Lord God of your grandfather Abraham and of your father Isaac, and I am going to give the land you are lying on to you and your descendants. They shall be as numerous as the dust of the earth, and through you all the families of the earth shall be blest."

From the beginning of time, men have been fascinated and impressed by dreams. The Hebrews believed they were messages from God. At a future time, Jacob's own son would be appealed to by a Pharaoh of Egypt for an explanation of the Pharaoh's dream. They are still studied by psychologists today, but in modern times they are considered the effect of actions already performed, not as predictions of things to come.

It is no wonder Jacob dreamed! Considering he was lying on the hard ground and the nature of his bed and pillow, a nightmare wouldn't have been surprising. But I think the subject of the dream had its roots in Jacob's own sub-conscious, born of his over-weening self-importance, having out-witted his father and his brother, stolen the precious birthright, and got off scot free. When he awoke, however, the effect of the dream was not pride but fear.

"Surely the Lord was in this place, and I knew it not!" he thought. "How dreadful is this place!"

Jacob's fear was a hopeful sign—it could have meant his conscience was stirring. Awake, sanity returned, and his unfounded self-confidence vanished. He was afraid of God. He presented a sorry spectacle as he hastily set up an improvised altar by pouring a little oil on some rocks, while making a self-serving promise, "*If* God will be with me, and will keep me *in this way that I go*, and will give me bread to eat and raiment to put on, so that I come again to my father's house in peace, *then* shall the Lord be my God."

God would have to make good first, before Jacob responded. Was there ever such an arrogant, one-sided arrangement offered to God? Oh yes—one other detail, a small bribe: "Of all that you give me, I promise to give one-tenth unto thee."

Probably feeling that he had done all that was needful to conciliate God, Jacob went on with his journey and came into the land of the people of the east. The first human beings he saw were men watering their sheep at a well. Using his best manners, Jacob addressed them.

"My brethren, where are you from?"

They answered, "We are from Haran."

"Do you know Laban, son of Nahor?"

"We know him."

"Is he well?"

The men said, "Yes, he is well. And here comes his daughter Rachel now, with their sheep."

There was a rather emotional meeting, as Jacob greeted his cousin and told her he was the son of Rebekah, her father's sister. She excitedly ran home with the news, leaving him and the sheep behind, but Laban returned with her to welcome his nephew and to bring him home. He had probably never expected to see his sister again, or any of her family, and he made Jacob very welcome.

After a month, during which Jacob had assisted Laban with his flocks, as a son would, Laban brought up the matter of wages, and asked Jacob to put a price on his services. (In the light of further revelations, I suspect Laban hoped by this means to keep Jacob with him permanently.) Laban, perhaps, expected him to mention so many sheep or goats as his price, but the young man surprised him.

"I'll take Rachel," he said.

Now Laban had another daughter, Leah, who was not very attractive, whereas Rachel was beautiful and well-favored. But Leah was older, and Laban preferred to marry her off first, so he hesitated.

"I will serve you for seven years for Rachel," said Jacob, and so Laban yielded and agreed.

Jacob carried out his part of this unusual bargain, and did it ungrudgingly. In fact, it didn't seem long, simply because he was in love and was a very happy man. But at last the time was up, the years of service were fulfilled, and Laban gave a big feast to which everyone on the place was invited, and there was rejoicing and merry-making. At last, when the marriage rites and the festivities were over, the happy bridegroom retired with his bride. But the girls were all heavily veiled, and Jacob did not learn until the next morning that Laban had not kept his part of the bargain. He had palmed off his unmarriageable daughter on his trusting nephew! Jacob was the sneaky type himself, but that didn't make it any better when such tricks were played on him! I don't envy Leah when Jacob discovered the deception or Laban either.

When Jacob had cooled down a little Laban said craftily, "Just let Leah have a week as your wife, and then you can have Rachel—provided you stay on and work for me seven more years."

And Jacob agreed. What else could he do? He still wanted Rachel. Though he had just learned that his father-in-law was a man without honor or integrity, that may not have bothered him excessively, except perhaps that he had been outsmarted. Actually, it was the last time that Laban got the best of Jacob.

As the years passed, Jacob's family increased by leaps and bounds. Leah had six sons and then a girl they called Dinah. Meanwhile, Rachel had borne none. Leah's attitude toward her own fruitfulness was that God sympathized with her because she was an unloved wife. Altogether, counting the contributions of his two concubines, Jacob had ten sons before poor Rachel finally produced Joseph. Some years later she had another little boy, Benjamin, but she died in childbirth.

After twenty years, Jacob decided he wanted to go back to Beersheba, to his father's home. In a final transaction, the division of the stock that constituted their wealth, Jacob managed to cheat Laban so badly that there was an open quarrel. They were a fine matched pair and deserved each other. There was only one difference: Jacob was smarter. And so, after all those years together, the separation was done in the spirit of ill will. The hostility of Laban and his sons was so great and so justified that Jacob decided to move out in the night. So he put his wives and sons on camels, and with all his goods and driving all his cattle, he slipped away secretly.

Laban didn't get the news until the third day. By that time he had missed some idols he valued, and he was angry enough to gather up the men of the family and start out in pursuit. Jacob, never dreaming that Nemesis was on his trail, was moseying along with his caravan when he heard the sound of many galloping hooves, and out of a cloud of dust emerged his angry relatives. Laban didn't waste time asking Jacob how he was, and whether he was having a good trip. He opened the conversation by demanding, "What do you mean by stealing out in the night and carrying away my daughters as if they were captives taken by the sword? It was rude and unnecessary! I would have given you a farewell party, with feasting and music. But you didn't even allow me to kiss my daughters and bid farewell to my grandsons! And worst of all, you have even *stolen my gods!*"

Jacob came back heatedly. "I slipped out because I didn't trust you! You would have sent me away empty-handed, keeping even my wives from me. As for your gods, I don't know anything about them. I certainly did not take them. So search if you want to, and if you find them the thief shall be punished."

Laban did search everywhere—the tents and the baggage— except Rachel's camel, upon which she was already seated and where the images were concealed. Then Jacob, who may have been as surprised as the crest-fallen Laban, as it was the sort of trick he could appreciate, launched into a self-righteous and not exactly true account of his stewardship of Laban's flocks and herds, finally summing up, "Thus have I been twenty years in thy house. I served thee fourteen years for thy two daughters and six years for thy cattle, and if the God of my father hadn't been with me, you would have sent me away empty-handed!"

By his angry retort, Laban then convicted himself and vindicated Jacob's fly-by-night exit, "These are *my* daughters, and their children are *my* children, and these cattle are *my* cattle, and everything in sight is *mine!*"

Now having gotten a good deal of meanness and rancor off their respective chests, they decided to accept the situation and to part in peace. so they made a pile of stones and called the place Mizpah, which means, "May the Lord watch between me and thee when we are absent one from another."

Early the next morning Laban kissed his daughters and grandsons and blessed them and started back to Haran.

Now, freed of Laban and a rich man, Jacob is still not a man at peace with himself. No man who has disregarded the laws of decency and humanity can ever be, for this is a moral universe. At this point, his past rose to haunt him. He began to think about his brother and how he had wronged him and to wonder uneasily if Esau had cooled off any in twenty years, or would still try to carry out his vow to kill Jacob. As he approached the country of Edom where Esau lived, he sent servants ahead to say to Esau, "We have come from thy brother with this message: 'I have been sojourning with Laban and stayed there till now. I have oxen, asses, flocks, men-servants, and women-servants. And these messengers I have sent to tell my lord, that I may find grace in thy sight.'"

The messengers returned with news that was anything but reassuring. "Thy brother Esau is coming to meet you with a force of four hundred men."

Jacob never for a moment entertained the idea that Esau might be coming in peace, for he knew what he deserved, and it was not a warm welcome. He didn't have four hundred men, or anything like it. If Esau attacked him, he would lose everything he had gained in twenty years, and maybe his life, too.

Fear is a great sharpener of perception. It can be like a flashlight turned on a situation that has been basking in the rosy glow of complacency. It jerked Jacob off his feet and onto his knees. That night he prayed, "O God of my father Abraham and Isaac, who said to me, 'Return to thy country and kindred, and I will deal well with thee,' I am not worthy of the least of all the mercies you have showed unto me. But deliver me, I pray thee, from the hand of my brother."

Then he took such action as he could. He divided his people and his cattle into two parts, and separated them, so that one half would have a chance to escape while Esau was engaged with the other. That was to be a last resort; he would first try bribery. So he rounded up 220 goats, twenty-two ewes and twenty rams, thirty milch camels with their colts, forty cows and ten bulls, twenty asses and ten foals. A servant was in charge of each group, and they were to encounter Esau not all at once but successively, to make the cumulative effect more impressive. Each time Esau met a servant with a herd, he would undoubtedly ask certain questions, "Who are you and whose are these herds?"

The servant was to answer, "They are a present to my lord from his brother Jacob."

Jacob was judging his brother by his own acquisitive spirit, and he had great hopes that such a present would melt a heart of stone. The size of the gift indicates the size of Jacob's fear.

That night, after the servants and the animals had gone, Jacob had a tremendous experience. He was alone. He moved his people and the rest of his stock across the ford Jabbok and settled them for the night, but he wasn't ready for sleep himself. He went back to the eastern side of the stream. "And there wrestled a man with him until the breaking of the day."

Who was this man? Jacob afterwards said, "I have seen God face to face." But we are told, "No man hath seen God at any time" (John 1:18).

"And he [the "man"] said, "Let me go, for the day breaketh," but Jacob said, "I will not let thee go, except thou bless me."

The man said, "Thy name shall be called no more Jacob but Israel, for as a prince hast thou power with God and with men and hast prevailed." And he blessed him there.

This was a description in physical terms of a spiritual experience. I think the man he wrestled with was himself, his better self, the man he could be. It was an experience that has happened over and over, to many men and woman. Kirkegaard once said, "There comes a midnight hour when every person must unmask." Sometimes the unmasking is done by another, forcibly, as when

Nathan the prophet went to a king on his throne and presented to that king a picture of himself as a defrauder, adulterer, and murderer. But perhaps more often it is done by conscience.

The midnight hour came to Jacob out in the desert the night before he met his brother, the man he had so grievously wronged, and I think it was caused by fear. His deeds stared him in the face. His conscience made a mockery of his wealth and possessions, for they accused him; they were not honestly or fairly won. He saw himself, probably for the first time in his life, as he really was— greedy, selfish, deceitful. His conscience told him he had to be right with God before he met his brother. The most graphic way to describe what went on in Jacob's soul that night is the one chosen—he "wrestled" with himself. The better nature was striving for the mastery; the natural man (the "old Adam") was determined on forgiveness and blessing.

After he had plumbed the depths of self-abasement, had had his baptism of suffering, he arose a new creature, a Prince of God, a man who had prevailed over his own sinful nature. He had a real spiritual awakening, much like Paul's, and it made a different man of him. Paul's was on the Damascus road at noon, in the blazing sun. Jacob's was at night, under the desert stars.

Even when sin has been forgiven, the consequences, like scars, remain. Jacob paid a high price for his past. He was crippled by it. Forever after, he "halted upon his thigh." I think the nervous strain he had been under may have brought on a mild stroke.

The story has a happy ending. Esau did arrive with four hundred men, but he ran to meet Jacob and hugged him, and the two men wept.

Then Jacob proudly presented his wives and children. When this interesting ceremony was over, Esau asked, "What is the meaning of all those droves of animals I kept meeting?"

"They are for you!" exclaimed Jacob. "I wanted you to be glad to see me."

I think Esau must have laughed at that, it sounded so boyish, but he said, "Keep them, my brother, for I have plenty of my own."

So they returned in peace to Canaan, where Jacob bought a piece of land for one hundred pieces of money and settled down with his family in Shechem. And he built an altar there unto the Lord.

Chapter 6

The Dreamer

Joseph

Part I

"Now Israel loved Joseph more than all his children."
Genesis 37:3

I think the story of Joseph is the most dramatic and suspenseful in the Old Testament. It is not just an almost incredible success story in the Alger tradition, though that alone would make it interesting. When I was a child, I read as many of Horatio Alger's books as I could get hold of—*Paul the Peddler, Phil the Fiddler,* and many others. Their names, luckily for the author, were just what he needed to make alliterative titles! My mother did not approve, as they did nothing to improve my literary taste, but since virtue always triumphed, she allowed my sister and me to read them.

There is far more in the story of Joseph than a boy making good. I find in it a corroboration of our belief that God is continually at work in the world, bringing good out of evil and converting trouble and pain into blessing.

It also provides some suggestive hints and warnings about family relationships and the interplay of human emotions. Many of the sins and weaknesses of human nature flourished in Joseph's home in Hebron. It was a family in which almost everything was done wrong. He was the apple of his mother's eye, to whom he had come late, and the spoiled darling of his father. So much indulgence would have been bad enough even if he had been an only son, but when he was one of thirteen children, it was a blunder of the first magnitude. Jacob had never concealed the fact that Joseph's mother, Rachel (who had died in giving birth to her second son, Benjamin) was the wife he really loved, a matter for deep-seated resentment by the ten sons of Leah and the concubines, and so he made those two, Rachel and Joseph, targets of the hatred and resentment of the rest of the family. He had a very colorful coat made for his favorite. It was a rare, if not unique, design, for many dyes were used to make the fabrics rich and beautiful. No wonder the half-brothers were jealous and resentful!

Joseph didn't help the situation. In fact, he contributed to the mess. At this period, I'm afraid he was unbearable, a silly vain boy, arrogant and boastful. He stirred up his brothers' jealousy and goaded them past endurance as he paraded his father's favoritism before them. He also talked too much. That's not a sin but is sometimes a mistake. That silent man, Calvin Coolidge, once observed, "What I never said never hurt me." A pity Joseph didn't have a little of that philosophy. The brothers knew he carried tales to their father, a habit that is not unusual for younger brothers but is not an endearing trait. He not only talked too much at the wrong time, but he said the wrong things. Perhaps he inherited his lack of tact from his father! At any rate, he added to his own unpopularity when he had some dreams that he boastfully related.

"Let me tell you about the interesting dream I had last night," he announced one morning. No one asked to hear it, but he told it anyway.

"We were out in the fields binding sheaves, each of us binding our own, and when we had finished, my sheaf stood up tall, and all your sheaves were in a circle around mine, and every one of your sheaves leaned over and made a low bow to mine! What do you think that means?"

The brothers' reaction was prompt and unmistakable. "If you think you're ever going to have dominion over us, you're crazy!"

That was bad enough, for the brothers' resentment was obvious, but a few days later he made things worse, for this time he offended his father.

"I had another dream," was his morning greeting. "I like this one even better. This time we were all stars. There were twelve of us, and your stars and the sun and moon all made obeisance to my star!"

This went beyond what even Jacob could tolerate, and he scolded his pet for his presumption. "Do you suggest that your mother and I and your brothers would ever under any circumstances bow down to you? Let's have no more of such nonsense."

I am not a psychologist, but I think I know why Joseph was so feisty and ill-conditioned. I suggest it was his brothers he wanted to impress, but he went the wrong way to work. He knew they didn't like him; they were a closed corporation from which he was excluded, and his little brother was probably too young for companionship. His father's favoritism was actually a handicap. Very convenient, at times, but I suspect he would have traded it to be accepted on equal footing by his older brothers. The family, of course, was his world, all the world he knew. Many a boy who had been excluded from some group should have some sympathy for Joseph.

It is not surprising that the intolerable situation exploded, for all the ingredients were present. Shortly afterwards his father sent Joseph to Shechem, where the young men were pasturing their flocks, to see how they fared. They had moved on to Dothan, but Joseph found them there. While he was some distance away, they recognized him—that wouldn't be hard since he was wearing his colorful coat—and the balloon went up.

"Behold, this dreamer cometh," one said bitterly. "Now's our chance. Let's take care of him here and now!"

Their hatred was so intense that there was not a dissenting voice until Reuben, the eldest, came up and heard what they were planning.

"What shall we do with him?" one asked.

"I say kill him and throw him into a pit. We can say a wild beast killed him and we discovered his body," was the inspiration of another.

Reuben knew that in their present frame of mind he wouldn't be able to talk them out of some act of vengeance, but he could talk them out of murder. He said, "No, no! We must not take his life. Shed no blood. Put him in one of these dry pits. It will be some time before he is found. That will give him a scare."

Reuben's plan was to linger till after they had all started homeward that evening and then to rescue his brash young brother.

We can imagine Joseph's sensations when he came jauntily up to the group, expecting to share their lunch with them, only to be seized, have his coat stripped off, and to be dumped roughly into a dry pit. While the men were eating, not far from a road that crossed the meadow, they saw a caravan coming. As they watched the approach of the camels, Judah said, "I have an idea. That caravan's going to Egypt—they may be merchants. Let's see if we can sell Joseph to them. That way we'll get something for ourselves." He added virtuously, "That will be better than to kill him. After all, he is our brother."

Unfortunately for Joseph, Reuben did not hear this callous scheme, and so it was carried out. The men on the camels were Ishmaelites from Midian on their way to Egypt with balm and myrrh and spices, and they were quite willing to invest in a healthy boy they could sell at a profit; so they paid the shepherds twenty pieces of silver, put Joseph on a camel, and went on their way.

Part II

Now let us follow Joseph to Egypt.

The principal reason this is a success story is that Joseph was both a dreamer and a doer. The prophet Joel wrote (2:28), "Your old men shall dream dreams and your young men shall see visions." He probably meant that the young men have the creative ideas and the old men have their memories. In common usage today, the words *dreams* rather than *visions* is used to mean ambitious plans and concepts. If he had never done anything but dream we would never have heard of Joseph, but his character had those two facets, the visionary and the practical.

We get a good view of his life as a whole as we look back on it from this twentieth century. We can see it was as full of ups and downs as a roller coaster. Circumstances slapped him down time after time, literally and figuratively—down into the dry pit, into

Egypt, into slavery, into prison. But each time he emerged triumphant, and each time he came closer to the fulfillment of his dreams. Some people are afraid to grasp opportunity when it comes, and as a result may lead ineffectual lives. But no sooner was Joseph on his own than the strength that was latent in his character began to grow.

In Egypt he was bought by a wealthy and important man named Potiphar, captain of the guard in Pharaoh's army. As far as he knew, he would spend the rest of his life in slavery, but he did not allow that depressing prospect to get him down. He just did the best he could in that degrading position. He was true to himself, his employer, and the God of his old father, and before long he had made an impression on his master. For he was so efficient in the performance of his duties and was such a handsome boy that Potiphar took a fancy to him and made him his steward. He was in complete charge of every aspect of the household. He handled the finances so wisely that Potiphar prospered. It was said that he, Potiphar, didn't even know what he had, what was bought or spent, because he was content to trust the young Hebrew who was such a fine manager.

Now it seems a pity that just when everything was running as smooth as glass that Fate once more slapped Joseph down. But all too often in this world, Edens have their snakes, for there are so many people that fill that role to perfection. This time his misfortune was not due to any fault in himself. Potiphar's wife was attracted by Joseph's looks and personality, and being without moral scruples or loyalty to her husband, she determined to carry on a clandestine affair with him right in her own home. One is proud of Joseph for staunchly refusing to take part in such an unworthy, shabby, dishonorable liaison. He tried to reason with the woman and to get her to see his point of view. "My master has trusted me with all that he has. It would be despicable of me to betray him."

She wasn't moved, and she didn't give up. She pursued him day after day. He avoided her as much as he could, but one day when there was no one else in the house she grabbed his garment. He knew he was in the presence of an evil temptress, and in a sort of panic he jerked away, leaving his garment in her hands, and left the house.

A woman scorned, it has been said, is a dangerous thing. It was certainly true in this case, for she took a mean revenge! She loudly claimed that Joseph had attempted to attack her, and her outraged cries had frightened him. He had fled, but she had his garment as evidence. What more did one need? Apparently Potiphar did not know his wife very well, for he believed her tale, and he had poor Joseph committed to prison. The knowledge that his kind master believed such a thing about him must have made this turn of events very hard to bear.

I wonder if Joseph as he sat there in his prison cell blamed God, if he was resentful and bitter and felt God had abandoned him. Some people in his place would have become cynical; they would have said, "What's the use in resisting temptation? I couldn't be any worse off!" The situation certainly looked hopeless, for he had no friends who might have tried to help him.

But Joseph kept up his courage and did not give way to despair. We know that, because after a while the chief jailer made him a trusty, and soured, bitter people are not given such responsibility. So he made friends there, which gave God something to work with. He could also use Joseph's interest in dreams and his talent for interpreting them. So it came about that when Pharaoh's chief butler and chief baker displeased the king and were arrested and put in prison, Joseph, naturally, became acquainted with them.

One morning, when Joseph in the performance of his duties entered their cell, they seemed more depressed than usual, so he asked, "What's the matter? Why do you look so sad?"

They both answered, "We each had a strange dream last night, and we're worried because we can't tell what they mean."

"Well, interpretations belong to God," Joseph said, "but tell me about them. I'm a dreamer myself. Maybe I can help."

The butler said, "In my dream I was standing near a grape vine that had three branches, and as I looked at it, it put forth buds that immediately bloomed, and the blooms became grapes. I had Pharaoh's cup in my hand, and I squeezed grape juice into it until I had filled the cup, and then I took it to Pharaoh."

Joseph thought a little while, and then said, "This is my interpretation. In three days, the king will pardon you and restore you to your office, and you will once more wait upon him as before."

The butler was ecstatic with this explanation, for he hadn't known whether he would ever get out of jail alive, and he showed no disposition to question Joseph's interpretation. Joseph didn't neglect this opportunity to help himself a little. When the butler's rapture had slacked off a bit, he said, "When you are back in the palace you could do me a good turn by telling the king I am in prison because I was unjustly accused. I have done nothing wrong." The butler promised he would tell the king.

Then the baker told his dream. "I thought there were three white baskets sitting on my head. The top basket was filled with food for Pharaoh, but a flock of birds swooped down and ate up all the food in the basket, and there was none left to carry to Pharaoh. What does that mean?"

This time Joseph said, "I'm afraid it's bad news. In three days Pharaoh is going to order your death by hanging."

Sure enough, three days later Pharaoh celebrated his birthday by a restoration and a hanging, just as Joseph had predicted.

But the chief butler, happily restored to favor, forgot Joseph and the promise he had made.

Two full years passed by with Joseph still in prison, perhaps marveling often at the ingratitude of human beings. Then the king had a dream. He was standing by the river and saw seven fine fat cows come up from the water and begin to graze in the nearby meadow. Soon seven lean hungry cows came up and ate the fat cows. He went back to sleep and had another dream which was very much like the first. He saw a corn stalk produce seven fine full ears. But at once seven thin, scanty ears came out, and they ate up the seven fat ears. When he woke and considered the two dreams, he didn't like them at all—they seemed ominous. He sent for all the magicians and wise men of Egypt and demanded an explanation, but none of them had any.

Then, finally, the chief butler remembered Joseph and was ashamed because he had forgotten his promise. He told the king about the dreams he and the chief baker had had in prison which had been interpreted by a young Hebrew and how they had both been fulfilled. Pharaoh lost no time in sending for Joseph. Delaying only to shave and change his clothes, the young prisoner was taken to Pharaoh.

When he had listened carefully to the dreams, Joseph said, "The wisdom to discover the truth is not in me, but in God. He will give the king an answer. He is showing you what he is going to do. The seven fat cows and the seven good ears are seven years of plenty. There will be good crops and bountiful harvests throughout Egypt. But they will be followed by seven years of famine, which will be very grievous unless preparation is made to avoid suffering. Let the king take advantage of this warning. Instead of squandering the crops during the prosperous years, let one-fifth be saved and stored against the famine which is sure to come. Appoint reliable agents who will faithfully execute this order. And then when hard times come, you and your people will have food.'"

Pharaoh and all who listened to this analysis were greatly impressed. The king turned to his advisers with a rhetorical question, "Whom do we have who can do the job as well as this young man who has devised it?" And to Joseph, "Since God has shown you all this, I trust your wisdom and discretion, and you shall be in charge of the whole project. You shall rule my house as steward. In authority you shall be next to me."

Joseph's sudden change of fortune with its attendant perquisites must have made his head swim, for Pharaoh put his own ring on his hand and called for a gold chain and fine linen garments to adorn him. He even selected a wife for him! As Joseph was now thirty years old and had had no opportunity even to meet any suitable girls, let alone fall in love, that seems like a very timely act on the part of the king.

So for the third time Joseph has been elevated to a position of responsibility, each new place superseding in importance the one before, and again he performed with distinction. A great deal of travel was involved, as he went all over Egypt supervising the gathering and storing of twenty percent of the abundant crops.

During those seven years he and his wife, Asenath, had two little boys who were named Manasseh and Ephraim. These were happy years.

The good times finally ended and yielded to famine. It was so severe and widespread that all the countries of the middle east were affected and the suffering became acute, but in all the land of Egypt there was bread. Now Joseph opened the storehouses, and there was plenty of corn and grain for the people to buy. There was even enough to spare for sale to the neighboring peoples, which saved many lives and put gold into the coffers of Egypt.

Now we approach the climax of Joseph's life. The famine that extended into Canaan, brought Joseph's brothers to Egypt on a quest for grain. Jacob, now an old man, did not go with them, nor did his youngest son, Benjamin. But all the ten older men went. Probably very few visiting delegations had any contact with the prime minister, as we might call him, but when Joseph learned that a group from his homeland composed of ten brothers had arrived to buy grain, he could have had little doubt as to who they were, so he had them brought into his presence.

They did not recognize him. He had been only a boy of seventeen when they saw him last. Now he was a man of thirty-nine, and he had changed greatly. Also, he was the last person they expected to encounter in the king's palace, robed in the finest and latest of Egyptian fashions (as I have no doubt he was). Awed by the splendor of their surroundings and the impressive official, they bowed low before him.

What an intriguing moment for Joseph! He thought of his boyish dreams when he had pictured his brothers making obeisance to him.

In order to get information about themselves, he pretended to believe they were spies and they protested vehemently that they were just what they seemed. "Thy servants are ten brothers, all sons of one man in the land of Canaan. And behold, the youngest is this day with our father, and one is not."

Joseph said, "I still believe you are spies. If you really have a young brother at home, he must brought here as proof that you are telling the truth. I will let nine of you go, with corn, but one must be left as hostage."

There followed a very emotional scene. Joseph had been speaking through an interpreter, so they thought he could not understand them, and they broke down and admitted to each other that this was God's punishment for their treatment of Joseph.

Reuben said, "Spake I not unto you, saying, 'Do not sin against the child,' and ye would not listen?"

This guilt must have lain heavy on their consciences all those years since they so promptly connected it with their present danger. Joseph was so moved that even while they were talking among themselves he went out, for he couldn't keep back the tears. He knew now that he had been mourned and his death regretted. It was a healing moment for him.

Then he gave private orders that each man's sack was to be filled with grain and his money also put in the sack, and they were to be provided with food for the return journey. But they were obliged to leave Simeon behind, in bonds.

At their first stop, at an inn, one of them opened his sack to feed his donkey and found his small bag containing his money! When he showed it to his brothers, all of them were uneasy. They didn't know what it meant and were frightened.

When they got home, they had a strange and disturbing story to tell their father. They did have grain, lots of it, but Simeon was in prison, and they feared they were in trouble. "The man who is the lord of the land spoke roughly to us, because he took us for spies. We said, 'We are true men—we are no spies,' and we told him about ourselves. When we mentioned Benjamin, he said if we would return and bring him, he would believe us and would release Simeon."

At that point they opened all the grain sacks and found that every man's money was inside his sack! Jacob saw only the dark side of this situation and mourned, "You have bereaved me of my children! Joseph is not, and Simeon is not, and ye will take Benjamin away."

Reuben exclaimed, "You may slay my two sons if I do not bring Benjamin safely home!"

But Jacob adamantly refused to agree to their taking Benjamin. It was not until all the corn was gone and the famine still raging that he was willing to consider it. Then he said, "Go again. Buy us a little food" Judah, for perhaps the dozenth time, said, "The man said positively we should not even get to see him unless our brother be with us." And Jacob, for perhaps the dozenth time, groaned, "Why did you tell the man you had another brother?"

Once again he got the answer, "The man asked us straight out, 'Is your father still alive? Have you another brother?' How could we know he would say, 'Bring your brother down'?"

Then, more gently, Judah said, "Send the lad with me and agree that we must go. If we don't, we will all starve. I will be surety for him. If I bring him not home to you, let me bear the blame forever."

So it was settled and they all set out, Jacob still so fearful that he insisted they take extra money to repay the man for the cash they had found in their sacks—"Maybe it was an oversight," he said nervously—and also an offering of such food as they had, honey, spices, nuts, and also myrrh. "And may God make him merciful so that he may release Simeon and permit you all to return with Benjamin," said the anxious father.

It was not a long journey down to Egypt, so perhaps he did not have to wait many days, but they seemed like months to the worried old man. So his joy and relief were in proportion to his anxiety when one wonderful day they returned, all eleven safe and sound, accompanied by wagons of provisions and ten asses loaded with corn and bread and meat! And what a story they had to tell!

First of all came the amazing news that their brother Joseph was not only alive but was governor over all the land of Egypt! It was he who had put the money in their sacks—it was no accident.

"We were treated like honored guests in his house. Our feet were washed—Simeon's, too—and then we were served a wonderful banquet! He was kind to all of us, but paid especial attention to Benjamin. Still none of us recognized him."

Then the men grew serious as they related the next part of their adventure, which had been no fun at all but rather had given them a terrible fright.

"The next morning we set out early, our asses carrying our sacks, but before we had gone far, servants of the governor overtook us and accused us of stealing a silver cup!"

Jacob was horrified at this turn of events. He cried, "Oh, no! You wouldn't have. . . ."

Judah didn't let the story lose any of its drama. "They searched our sacks," he said impressively, "beginning with Reuben and going down the line"—Jacob was holding his breath—"and they found it—in Benjamin's sack."

Benjamin said nothing, but he was enjoying the tale.

"Well, we went back, and I told the governor how reluctant you had been to let your youngest son go, and how I had made my life surety for his safe return."

Judah had indeed made a very moving plea: "We have a father, an old man, and a child of his old age, a little one; and his brother is dead, and he alone is left of his mother, and his father loveth him." He described the whole situation in their home and then finished, "Now therefore I pray thee, let me remain as a bondman instead of the lad, and let him go up with his brethren. For how shall I go up to my father if the lad be not with me?"

He paused. Jacob cried, "Yes, yes—Go on!"

"Well, he sent all the servants out, and then, speaking in Hebrew, he said, 'I am Joseph, your brother whom you sold to Midianites when I was a boy. Don't you know me now?' But we didn't, and we still couldn't believe it! *Joseph alive!* Then he began to weep, and so did we all. Before we could even ask his forgiveness he said, 'Do not be angry with yourselves, for God's hand was in it. He did send me before you to preserve life.' Then he told us the famine would go on for five more years. He wanted us to come home just to pack up and get you and then move to Egypt to be near him, for he said, 'The good of all the land of Egypt is yours'."

Others took up the tale, supplying details Judah had left out. They told how interested the Pharaoh had been. "It was he who said we must have wagons to carry back our goods—all because he thinks so highly of our brother, for it was Joseph whose good management and wisdom saved Egypt!"

What a grand climax! Not only the brothers but the author made the most of it.

I feel that Joseph's idea that God had planned his whole career, with its vicissitudes, hardships, and even suffering, was in reality the interpretation of the author of this story as he looked back, as we have done and saw how consistently the defeats and disappointments and seeming disasters proved to be stepping stones to better things. But Joseph's own conduct—his integrity, his self-discipline, his courage—were necessary for the victories he won. God provided the opportunities, and Joseph seized them.

Every life contains circumstances that can become stumbling blocks or stepping stones, depending on what we do about them. "The worst turns the best to the brave." I think St. Paul would accept as a suitable translation of a sentence he wrote to the Christians in Rome, *"All things can be worked together for good."* I think God never *wills* suffering for any purpose. He works continually not to *prevent* but to *defeat* suffering. Mephistopheles in Goethe's *Faust* says bitterly, "I am the spirit who, willing evil, forever creates good." How frustrating for him!

God is the Spirit who wills good and who works with willing human hearts and hands to achieve it.

Chapter 7

The Ambitious Woman

Miriam

She had such a lovely name! Miriam. So different from the strange ones like Zipporah and Keturah and Zeresh, which are unfamiliar and, therefore, unlovely.

She had talent, too, and force of character. She had status and influence, for she was the only sister of the leader of the nation. So it is saddening to find her a most unlovely person.

To make it even more disappointing, she had been such an interesting child! She was a little girl when the terrible Time of Trouble came. By order of the Pharaoh of Egypt, all the baby boys of the Hebrew people were to be drowned in the Nile at birth.

Could this be the same Egypt where Israel and his family had been received so warmly and where they had lived in peace and security along with the Egyptians? The same country, yes, but many things had changed. Year had passed, a whole generation had died, and "a Pharaoh arose who knew not Joseph." Probably he had never heard of him nor how it came about that the richest section of the country was peopled by an ethnic group who were united closely and had their own religion. This Pharaoh was afraid of the growing strength of the people who lived within the borders of his country. They were treated like slaves, The danger of an uprising does not seem to have been very real, but tyrants are always afraid of even imaginary threats. The proclamation struck terror to every Hebrew home, for all would be affected in some way by the cruel order.

In Miriam's home there was a plump rosy-cheeked baby boy, the pride and pet of the whole family. Fiercely determined that her baby should not be sacrificed, the mother, Jochabed, made a little boat of rushes, just big enough to hold a baby, lined it with water-repellent tar and pitch, and anchored it in the river under the over-hanging bushes on the bank. When Pharaoh's soldiers came along the street to the sound of screams and moans from the stricken families, Miriam's little brother was sleeping peacefully in his cradle on the river.

He had to be kept hidden, under the watchful care of some member of the family, till all danger was past. It happened to be the little sister's turn when something occurred that had not been anticipated. Pharaoh's daughter came to the river to bathe and chose the very spot where the small craft was moored. From her hiding place Miriam saw the waiting women lift the little boat from the water and hold it while the princess gazed delightedly at the sleeping child. There was a little consternation when he woke up and began to cry, so Miriam ran forward. She heard the princess say, "This is one of the Hebrew children. I'm going to save him."

An even older person than Miriam might have been in a quandary about what to do, but the quick-witted child was not at a loss.

"Would you like for me to get a nurse for the baby?" she asked politely.

The princess was pleased with the suggestion, and off Miriam flew to her mother with the disconcerting news that the tiny boy had been discovered by—of all people—the daughter of the Pharaoh!

When Miriam returned with her anxious mother, the princess was still smiling at the little boy in her arms. "I shall call him Moses," she said, "Because I drew him from the water." Then she handed him over to the "nurse," who was to keep him during his infancy.

Jochabed must have been very fearful that the princess' human intention might prove fleeting or that if the presence of a Hebrew boy at court became known he would be taken from her by force. But whether the secret was well-kept, or whether the Pharaoh, her father, decided one boy would do no harm, especially one under his own eye, the boy was accepted. Although for some years he remained under the care and influence of his own mother, he became known as the son of Pharaoh's daughter.

In his little boyhood he was taken to the court, where he grew to manhood. Although he was reared in luxury and exposed to nothing higher than the ideas and conduct of a pagan environment, he remained remarkably unaffected. I believe he is a good example of the power of an early influence, for the pampered life at a sybaritic court did not stifle his native loyalties, or extinguish the remnants of the Jehovah-worship that Jacob's son, Joseph, had brought to Egypt. Had his mother, like Hannah, the mother of Samuel, been able to implant in his childish mind the seeds of ideals of justice and humanity? It must have been so. The seeds germinated, and one day there was an explosion. The pressure had been building up as he witnessed instances of cruelty to Hebrew men by the Egyptian overlords, as he must have done, and suddenly the resentment he had been feeling became a tempestuous fury, and before he knew what he was going to do, he had killed an Egyptian.

All that rash act accomplished was to cause Moses to run for his life. Convinced that he would not be safe anywhere in Egypt, he fled to Midian, where a new and very different life began for him. The first people he met were the seven daughters of the priest of Midian. He had stopped at a well, when the girls came to water their father's sheep. But just as they had drawn some water, a group of rough, rude shepherds came up and tried to drive the girls away. But Moses stood up, took over the bucket, and told the shepherds he was helping the girls and the men could just wait their turn. Which they did. This is the second incident where we see Moses championing the helpless, even at some risk to himself.

When the girls got home, their father, Jethro, asked, "How is it that you are come so soon today?"

They said, "There was a young man at the well, an Egyptian, and when the shepherds tried to drive us away, he prevented them, and then he watered our flocks!" It was quite an adventure in their quiet lives, and they were full of it.

When he could get a word in, Jethro asked, "Well, where is the young man? Do you mean you just came off and left him? Go back and invite him to come and eat with us."

So Moses, like another man who came to dinner, stayed on at the invitation of Jethro, and became his shepherd and eventually his son-in-law, for he married one of the daughters. Her name was Zipporah.

For some years Moses led a quiet pastoral life. I do not think, however, that it was a contented life. He had recognized the deplorable conditions in Egypt that cried out to him for change, but he had run from them. This knowledge wouldn't let him rest. In the fields with the sheep all day, there was nothing to occupy him but his thoughts, and they kept him busy. It is not surprising that God was able to get his attention and tell him what he wanted him to do.

Finally, after many excuses and much arguing with his conscience, Moses reluctantly went back to Egypt, dedicated to the super-human task of liberating his countrymen, the Hebrews. His first step was to locate his brother Aaron and his sister Miriam to get their cooperation and to make plans for getting their people out of Egypt, with Pharaoh's permission, if possible. If not, without it.

I think Pharaoh may have been amused when he first learned of this scheme. Give up their slaves? What an idea! It was laughable.

He didn't laugh long, however. How it was done is a long story and full of drama. It inspired one of the most popular of the Negro spirituals, "Let My People Go." It is also very familiar, so it is not necessary to review it here. It can be read in Exodus, Chapters 3 through 13.

Let us go on to the place where Miriam re-enters the story. If we have been expecting that she, like Aaron, would help her brother in his tremendous undertaking to free a rabble of slaves and then to meld them into a nation, we are doomed to disappointment. She could have been a great help to him, Oh my, yes! The alert, poised, self-confident little girl had become a strong-minded forceful woman. She was talented, too. When the Egyptians drowned in the Red Sea, she composed a victory song, a song of wild rejoicing and triumph, for the women to sing, so she was considered a poet and a musician, and this gave her prestige in her own right. She could easily have been the recognized leader of the women and have mobilized them behind Moses when the people grumbled at the hard desert life and questioned his authority.

But, sad to say, that role did not satisfy her. She was not interested in strengthening and supporting her brother. She had become aggressively ambitious on her own account and was interested in promoting herself at his expense. How she did debase that beautiful word *sister*! She was evidently jealous of his position, for she was not satisfied just to promote herself—she tried to tear him down. Do you remember how she went about it? She started a whispering campaign against him, one of those sly secret attacks that are hard to counter because the harm is done before the victim can discover the source, or even what the whisper is. Miriam seized on Moses' second marriage as a means to stir up resentment against him, for he had married an Ethiopian woman. Zipporah had gone back to Midian, by either her own wish or Moses'. Maybe she tired of the desert life and went back to her father and sisters.

The resentment was not due to the same kind of race prejudice that we are familiar with. In that part of the world, where all complexions were shaded from brown to black, white skin was definitely not a mark of superiority. The only way in which white was used in the Old Testament to refer to skin was in connection with leprosy. The Queen of Sheba was Ethiopian and was considered a great beauty. But there was strong nationalistic feeling, and it operated the same way.

Miriam's mean little campaign against her brother did him some harm, but while she was waiting for that poison really to take effect, she took another step. This one was intended to elevate herself instantly to a position of power, but this proved her undoing: she anointed herself a prophetess! Her idea was that when her secret attack had undermined Moses' authority, she would be already ensconced in a position of unassailable power. She would be, in today's terms, head of both Church and State. But she outsmarted herself. The whole astonishing episode is told in Numbers 12:1–16.

God had not been indifferent to what was going on. He was very angry with Miriam for her treatment of Moses, and her assumption of the role of prophetess was the last straw. At that point, he took action. He spoke "suddenly" to Moses, Aaron, and Miriam, "Come out to the tabernacle of the congregation, all three of you." When they had obeyed, he came down in a pillar of cloud and stood in the door of the tabernacle. The children of Israel were still thinking of him as a physical being who had to hide himself by some means from their eyes.

His first words were to Miriam, and they were a stern rebuke for naming herself a prophetess. That was a religious title, and she had no right to it. "If anyone is to be a prophet," God said, "I'll be the one to tell her—or him. I'll do it in a vision or a dream. I have not appeared to *you*! With my servant Moses I speak face to face, and clearly. Not in obscure speeches."

This seems to imply that God didn't think much of prophetesses, who, like oracles, had to be figured out! With one final angry utterance—"Wherefore, then, were ye not afraid to speak against my servant Moses?"—God departed in the cloud. When the cloud was gone, it was discovered that Miriam was a leper "as white as snow." It wasn't in the early stages—she was a terminal case!

But Aaron pled for her to Moses (Aaron's conscience couldn't have been too easy, for he was involved to some extent in Miriam's plot), and Moses cried unto the Lord. He didn't hesitate an instant—he begged the Lord to forgive Miriam and to heal her. But God *did* hesitate! At this period in their history, the Hebrews had endowed him with very human characteristics. It is plain to be seen that he had no enthusiasm for this act of mercy. He said grudgingly, "Well, shut her outside the camp for seven days, and after that you can let her come in."

If this were the best picture or the final revelation we had of God, we wouldn't learn much about forgiveness from him. But it is a fascinating study to trace the Hebrews' spiritual growth. We know, now, that that quick compassion of Moses for his disloyal sister was his most God-like quality. By the time the earliest psalms were written, they had so grown in understanding that those songs are full of such lines as "The Lord is merciful and gracious, slow to anger and plenteous in mercy." That idea represents a great change from Moses' time.

I have wondered what effect that horrifying experience had on this ambitious woman. Was she bitter and resentful? Or deeply thankful that she had been spared a terrible fate? I could find only three further references to her in the Old Testament. The first tells that Miriam died in Kadesh and was buried there (Num 20:1). She is mentioned in a genealogy as one of the three children of Amram (1 Chron 6:3). Finally in Deuteronomy 24:9, in the enumeration of laws and punishments, we read, "Remember what the Lord thy God did unto Miriam by the way, after ye were come forth out of Egypt." So this talented, high-placed woman who could have done so much to serve God by helping her brother, and who could have had an honored place with great women of the past, exists in religious history only as a warning, "Remember what happened to Miriam. . . ."

I find her very pathetic. There is nothing wrong with ambition unless it is misdirected. She wanted to be great, but she had the wrong idea about what greatness is and how to attain it. We can all think of some figures in public life today who have made the same mistake—confused greatness with prominence and social recognition and, most dangerous of all, with power. One of the most important lessons in life and the hardest to learn is that the qualities of greatness are self-forgetfulness, humility, and service for humanity.

Some valuable guidelines have been given us by two noted men. Woodrow Wilson said, "No man is great who thinks himself so, and no man is good who does not strive to secure the happiness and comfort of others."

In the words of Leo Tolstoy, "There is no greatness where there is not simplicity, goodness, and truth."

Chapter 8

A Visit from an "In-Law" and Its Consequences

Moses and His Kin

When Moses finally got the children of Israel out of Egypt and across the Red Sea, his problems and troubles weren't over. His biggest one was solved, but he had plenty of new ones. He had on his hands a rabble of people with no organization, no civic ideas or training, and no understanding of what their deliverer had in mind for them.

When I was a small Sunday School child, very familiar with the expression "the children of Israel" but never enlightened as to what it meant, I had the idea that they were about my age and that they were lost for years and years and wandered around in the desert having a miserable time because they couldn't find the way to Palestine! Well, they were pretty miserable at times, but they weren't lost. Although they were no longer slaves and should have felt their freedom was worth all it cost, they found plenty to complain about, and complain they did! They missed the life and ways and food they were used to. Particularly the food! Oh, for the beautiful melons of Egypt! Oh, for the leeks and the cucumbers and the garlic! If they had known they were leaving the flesh-pots! There was the horrible climate—too dry and too hot, and there was too much sand in everything! The fact is, they were homesick. Their roots were deep in Egyptian soil, and pulling up roots is always painful.

Along with the physical hardships, there was the new religion to be accepted and understood. In Egypt they had taken the course of least resistance and adopted the local gods, Isis and others, gods made of stone and metal and wood. Perhaps the hardest part of Moses' task was to substitute an invisible God for deities that could be seen and touched.

Moses was nearly distracted with the real problems and the imaginary complaints. He was not getting any cooperation, just reproaches and criticism, and he was swamped with these. Everything was brought to him, and he tried to resolve every difficulty and settle every complaint, which was an impossible task. Every day he was getting further behind. Something had to be done!

He did not at first recognize his relief when it came, for it was in the person of his father-in-law, Jethro, a man who was not involved in any way in Moses' plans. He would make only a short visit, and was not even a Hebrew. He had come from his home in Midian to bring Moses' wife, Zipporah, and his two sons to him. At some point, she, with the boys, had gone home to her father. The explanation is guess work: she may have gotten tired of the desert life, or—a nice reason—Moses may have sent his family to Midian for their safety during the critical stage of what was undoubtedly a very hazardous adventure. It is even possible that if the boys were particularly lively or obstreperous, he might have felt that he had enough on his hands without having to cope with them as well!

The arrival took Moses by surprise, and his delight comes across to us as we read, notwithstanding the great age of the musty, dry-as-dust account. The author passes over the to-be-expected hugs and kisses for wife and sons and mentions the warmth of his welcome to Jethro.

After the tired mother and children were in bed, Moses and Jethro talked far into the night, for there was much to tell. Moses had a tremendous message to report, the whole story of his triumph over Pharaoh, and how Jehovah had directed and sustained him every step of the way. The tale was a stirring one, and it moved Jethro deeply.

"Blessed be the Lord," he exclaimed, "who hath delivered you out of the hand of the Egyptians and out of the hand of Pharaoh! Now I know that the Lord is greater than all gods."

The next day Jethro made a burnt offering to Jehovah, just as if he had been a Hebrew instead of a Kenite, an action that was very pleasing to Moses. It was followed by a dinner in his honor, to which some of the chief men, "elders of Israel," were bidden.

It did not bother Moses in the least that his father-in-law had said Jehovah was the "greatest of all gods" not "the only God," because that is what Moses himself thought. The time when Jehovah would be recognized by Jews as the one God of the universe was hundreds of years in the future. Their plan, to drive the inhabitants out of Palestine and take it for their homeland, a goal which motivated them during their forty years in the desert, was based on their belief that he was their God alone and only they were his people. The Philistines, who would be their enemies when they got there, were also God's enemies. They were still living with this misconception as late as David's time; when Saul drove David out of the country, a large part of David's misery was due to the idea that he was outside Jehovah's jurisdiction. "They said to me, 'Go serve other gods!'" (1 Sam 26:19).

I think Moses enjoyed his father-in-law's visit very much, even if only for social and domestic reasons, but he did not know it was to have far-reaching consequences and that he was soon to have cause to be eternally grateful to him. During the next several days, Jethro observed the daily life of the encampment. He watched Moses as he engaged in his hopeless task of trying to dispense justice and settle disputes, falling further behind his work load every day. Finally, just before he started back to his home in Midian, he had a conference with his son-in-law in which he gave him some excellent advice.

He said, "Moses, you've got to stop doing everything yourself. That isn't a good system. You're wearing yourself out and the people too, and you're not getting the job done."

Moses acknowledged that it did seem to be a hopeless task. "But what else can I do?"

"I'll tell you what you can do. You can get men to help you. You can delegate some of these cases to others. You've got some good men here. Select the best ones and give them some responsibility. I suggest you divide your people into groups of one thousand families. Then sub-divide these into one hundred, and fifty, and finally ten families. There should be a leader for each group, with the best men in the top jobs, of course. The big matters they will naturally bring to you, but many small matters can be solved by your agents, and this will be good for everyone."

Moses nodded in full agreement as his father-in-law talked. But Jethro wasn't through. He had given this plan serious thought before he spoke, and he had some ideas about the qualifications of the men Moses would need. "Select men who will make honorable and trustworthy leaders," he said. "Men who fear God, love truth, and hate covetousness."

He knew that a man who guards against covetousness will never take the first step toward greed and bribery and corruption, traits that have been the undoing of all too many men in positions of trust.

What Jethro did not say was interesting, too. He did not say, "Choose clever men, those who are popular, who know how to exert pressure here and there to get things done quickly." You notice he expressed no fears about the men being competent to do the work. Once selected and instructed, he was confident they would rise to the occasion. Generally, when care has been taken to fit the person to the job, and especially when that person possesses the characteristics Jethro suggested, he or she *will* rise to the occasion.

Margaret Lee Runbeck, in *The Great Answer*, told a true story that illustrates graphically the fact that in most cases responsibility brings growth, and duties bravely undertaken generate the strength necessary to perform them. A young American girl, whose first name was Margot, married a Frenchman before World War II. When France fell, he was taken prisoner and sent off to one of the horror camps in Germany. Margot knew her own situation was extremely dangerous. She must get home to America with their little daughter, Rose Helene, three years old, but she had almost no money. Her only idea was to get to the Spanish border and cross the Pyrenees. So she got train tickets to a little town on the edge of France. There, she began asking questions in whispers.

She learned that there was a little group of brave humanitarians who were helping refugees cross the mountains into Spain. She made a contact with one of these, a man, who told her how and where to meet a group up in the mountains who were ready to cross over. But he said, "You will have to leave the child. She couldn't make it."

She answered, "The child is my strength. I could not take one step without her."

He shrugged fatalistically. Perhaps he thought, "It doesn't matter too much how one dies."

They had breakfast, Margot and her little one; then they set out across the meadow that was at the foot of the nearest mountain. They had climbed up the mountain only a few hundred feet when they met snow and wind. Rose Helene's little coat was too short. Her patent leather slippers were soon soaked. Margot wrapped the little feet in her own scarf and carried her. They managed to find the shelter where the other refugees waited, slept a few hours, and all together set out at 5 A.M. Five o'clock on a December morning in the Pyrenees!

It took four endless days and nights to struggle over the pass. The leader at the shelter had been aghast when he saw the child, but Margot said, "She can do anything she needs to do." And so it proved. Instead of being a burden, she was what kept them going. It was an adventure to her, and she laughed and chatted to whoever carried her, for they all began to take turns relieving Margot. Sometimes one would give up, drop down in the snow, say, "I can go no farther. You'll have to leave me—it doesn't matter."

The first time this happened, the leader was inspired to say, "You can't give up now! It's your turn to carry the child." The poor fellow struggled to his feet. He would first do his duty—then die.

Those two dropped behind, but soon the rest heard them talking, heard Rose Helene's silvery little laugh, and knew the discouraged one was himself again. No—he was more than himself! After that, they always made the weakest one carry the child till his strength and will were restored.

Jethro's advice, with its emphasis on spiritual qualities for leadership and with its significant omissions, is timely in our twentieth century. My husband and I once sat behind two preachers on a train who were returning from a state meeting of their church. One of them was doing nearly all the talking, although he did pause occasionally for brief answers to his questions. He kept calling the church his "plant."

"What's the size of your plant? How many buildings does your plant have? My plant has. . . ."

I found myself expecting to hear the plant's whistle blow!

Then he started on money. "What's your debt? How much equity? How much money did you raise last year? How much did you raise for this? for that? How many members do you have?"

Although it wasn't any of my business, and he wasn't even talking to me, he kind of rubbed me the wrong way. Then he put the clincher on my disapproval when he said, "Sometimes I have to practice a little 'fassi-ism' on my deacons to get my program through. If I didn't, they'd wreck it!"

"*Fassi-ism!*" He didn't even know how to pronounce it. He was doing just what Jethro warned Moses against—running a one-man show, using his power to push. He never said, "God's program," or even "the church's program," but "my program." God doesn't work that way. Jesus only stood at the door and knocked; he didn't push it open.

I think Moses took a big stride forward when he listened respectfully, even humbly, to Jethro's advice and accepted his suggestions. He did not dismiss them as the ideas of a mossback because Jethro was an older man, nor scorn them because he was a "foreigner." He didn't resist them because they were not his own, or because they were the notions of an in-law, a group which, like prophets, doesn't always enjoy status.

Then Jethro, having (without realizing it) put his stamp indelibly on the Hebrew people, returned to his home in Midian. He had helped Moses establish a democratic government *under God*, for Jehovah was the recognized head. It was a complete union of Church and State. Government and religion were one. (After Moses died, there was a period when they were ruled by judges, some good and some bad, and then in Samuel's time they demanded a king.)

Isn't Jethro a rather delightful old man? Isn't it surprising to find he had a spiritual nature as real as Moses' own? It shouldn't surprise us, though it should remind us, that God speaks to anyone who will listen, not just to those who belong to our groups and who use the same religious terms that we do. Jesus said, reproving his disciples for just such a narrow concept, "Other sheep I have which are not of this fold."

Even before Jesus came, Cicero, the Roman philosopher, made a beautiful statement that God alone must have put into his mind: "True law is right reason, consonant with nature, everlasting and unchanging. It does not differ for Rome or Athens, or for the past, present, or future. No legislature can repeal it or relieve us of the obligations that it imposes, and one need not look outside oneself for the true Expounder of it."

Cicero would not have used the term "holy Spirit" if he had identified the source of the true law, but he referred to the only one who can communicate with the spirit inside each of us. It is enough that Cicero recognized his existence.

When my mother was a girl, she spent a year in New York studying art. The year was 1886. One day she went to a religious meeting where the speaker was a young Japanese woman about 35 years old. She was the first woman lawyer in Japan. Her father had been a poet, a nominal member of one of the heathen religions. He had never heard of Christianity, but he said often to his daughter, "There is something else, some truth this religion does not have. There are questions this religion does not answer. You must look for something higher. Do not rest until you have found it."

He died without learning what it was. When his daughter heard of a religion called Christianity, she went to learn about it, and when she was told the story of a God who so loved the world that he sent his son to teach it about God and about Love, she knew that was it—the thing her father had hungered for. Though he was not formally a Christian—how could he be?—the promise Jesus made, "Whoever hungers and thirsts after righteousness shall be filled," applied to him, and I like to think of the warm welcome he got when he arrived at his Father's house.

Perhaps Jethro met him there.

Chapter 9

A Man of Valor

Gideon

One of the most dramatic stories in the Old Testament is related in Judges 6, 7, and 8. It has everything—lively, rapid narration, suspense, humor, and a happy ending. It also has an interesting plot concerning a tough problem and a situation in which the good guys are badly outnumbered by the bad ones.

This story should have an appeal for boys because it is an action story, and is not unlike science fiction. But girls can enjoy it, too. When I was a small girl and was allowed to play outdoors on summer evenings until dark with the other children of the neighborhood, we sometimes acted out Bible stories. One I enjoyed was Gideon and the Midianites. Our house was next to a vacant lot with a grove of trees on it and a natural slope in the rear, so the lower level was perfect for the valley where the Midianites lived and where they were sleeping when surprised by Gideon's troops. There is one fly in the honey of my nostalgic recollections: I never made Gideon's band. Being small and unheroic of stature, I always had to be a Sleeping Midianite!

The hero of this story was a plain young man, not a king, or outstanding in any way. Just a farmer. It must have been easy for little Hebrew boys to identify with him when the story was told them. (Let's remember that these stories were told, not written, for many generations.) He was practical, shrewd, and far from gullible. He even demanded proof of an angel!

Our sympathies are stirred at once as we read about the cruel rapacious Midianites who were terrorizing Israel. There were Bedouin tribes from beyond Jordan, and they would dash over on their camels, seize cattle and crops, and go back to their tents until the Israelites had another crop ready to harvest. Then, like locusts or vultures, they would swoop again, stealing what they wanted and destroying the rest.

The Israelites were just taking it, for they were not organized and had no military leader. So they were protecting themselves in the only way they knew—living in caves and dens in the mountain and trying to raise in secret enough food to keep themselves and their animals alive.

The author of the tale said that God was punishing Israel for its sins. I wonder, if he had been living in one of those caves with the rest, wondering where his next meal was coming from, or even if there was going to be a next meal, whether he wouldn't have felt that the punishment did not fit the crime but rather was cruel and excessive. But it would be many generations before the Hebrews would even begin to have an understanding of Jehovah as a God of love.

They were wrong about something else too—he had not deserted them.

There was a young man named Gideon, the son of Joash, who lived in the community of Ophrah. One day he was in his winepress, threshing wheat by hand and getting the chaff all over him. The normal way of threshing grain was to use oxen or horses to tread it out and to do it on top of a hill or elevation where the wind would carry the chaff off as it left the stalks; but that practice had been abandoned, for it would have been an invitation to the Midianites to come right over and help themselves.

As I say, Gideon was threshing when he had an unusual visitor: an angel came by to see him. The heavenly guest sat down under a nearby oak tree.

The stage is now set for one of the funniest scenes in the Old Testament. I can imagine old Hebrew grandfathers telling it in solemn tones but with twinkling eyes.

Gideon didn't even pause in his work. He treated the angel like a neighbor stopping by to borrow something. The angel opened the conversation with a compliment for Gideon.

"The Lord is with thee, thou mighty man of valor."

So far, Gideon hadn't done anything more valorous than plow and hoe and manage to stay alive, so this remark was a hint that he was going to do something, and a bit of flattery to help the angel put it over.

Gideon wasn't impressed. "Oh, yes?" he said. "If the Lord is really with us, why has all this misery befallen us? What about all the miracles that he performed for our forefathers? According to them! He has certainly forsaken us, and left us at the mercy of the Midianites."

Seeing that his task wasn't going to be easy, the Lord had to drop his disguise.

"*You* are going to save Israel from the Midianites. Go in the power of your youth and strength. Have not *I* sent you?"

Gideon was skeptical. "How am I going to save Israel? I'm the poorest man in the poorest family in the smallest tribe." (It was the tribe of Manasseh.)

There is more than a touch of bitterness in this speech, for wealth was considered a sign of God's favor.

God brushed that excuse aside. "But I will be with you."

He did not say, "You are young, strong, popular. People will follow you. It won't be so hard." He said only, "*I* will be with you." That would make all the difference.

Gideon was not convinced. He asked for a sign—as if he hadn't already had one!

"Will you wait while I prepare a present for you?" he asked.

The Lord said yes, he would wait. So Gideon went to the house and prepared a kid for roasting, and he made some small unleavened loaves of bread. He put the meat in a basket and the broth from it in a pot and brought them, with the bread, out to the oak tree.

"And the angel of the Lord put forth the end of the staff that was in his hand and touched the flesh and the unleavened cakes; and there rose up fire out of the rock and consumed the flesh and the unleavened cakes. Then the angel of the Lord departed out of his sight."

Convinced at last that Jehovah had singled him out to save Israel, Gideon began that very night. With ten of his own trusted servants to help, he harnessed a young bullock and overturned the altar of Baal, which his own father had erected, and then cut down the "sacred" grove in which it stood. By doing this at night, he was able to present his father and the other Baal-worshiping men of the town with a *fait accompli*. Now he had to face the consequences, and they were serious. The men demanded that Joash bring his son out to be killed, and if Joash had not supported his son, he would have been. But the father's best instincts were aroused.

"Do you plead for Baal?" he asked the angry men. "If he be a god, let him plead for himself!"

So the men backed down. But the Midianites and the Amalekites began massing for war in the valley of Jezreel. Gideon responded by sending messengers throughout Manasseh, and also to the nearby tribes of Asher, Zebulun, and Naphtali, with a call to arms. His countrymen did not fail him; volunteer fighting men came. But on the verge of war, Gideon's heart failed him. He was no soldier, yet he had to conduct the battle that was inevitable. Once more he appealed for a sign.

"And Gideon said unto God, 'If thou wilt save Israel by mine hand, as thou hast said, I will put a fleece of wool on the floor, and if in the morning the dew be on the fleece only, and the floor around it be dry, then shall I know that thou wilt save Israel by mine hand, as thou hast said'."

And that is what happened. Gideon, nervous and frightened, must have crept out at dawn to check that fleece, and when he had squeezed it out, he had a bowl full of water!

Well, that seems like a good healthy sign. But we can judge the condition of Gideon's nerves by the fact that he wasn't satisfied.

"Please don't be angry with me," he prayed, "but grant me just one more proof! Let the fleece be dry, while the ground is damp with dew."

So God humored him. The next morning, the fleece was dry, but I wouldn't be surprised if Gideon needed overshoes to wade out to where it lay!

Finally, unable to postpone his surrender any longer, Gideon agreed to be God's agent. The first step God told him to take was to reduce his forces, "for I want it understood, when I deliver the Midianites into your hands, that the victory was not by man's might but by my power." He told Gideon to announce to the army that all who had been conscripted against their wills and were afraid to fight for Israel were free to go home. Twenty-two thousand men immediately turned tail. This left only ten thousand, but they were brave men.

But God said, "That's still too many. Bring them to the river to drink, and keep the ones that sip the water from their hands. Dismiss the ones that lap like a dog." This process eliminated all but three hundred. God said, "With this three hundred men will I save you and deliver Midian into thy hand."

"And the host of Midian was beneath him in the valley." That sentence has an ominous sound, and the fact was certainly ominous to Gideon. He could see the tents of the enemy, and they were like grasshoppers for multitude, and their camels were like the sands of the seashore. Truly an awe-inspiring sight! Once more he felt his confidence and courage draining away.

Then he had an idea. Actually, it was God's suggestion. He would infiltrate the enemy camp and see if he could pick up any useful information. That very night he took his trusted servant, Phurah, and under cover of darkness they stealthily crept close to one of the outlying tents. This took a good deal of daring, for their lives wouldn't have been worth a plugged nickel if they had been discovered. As they drew near, they heard a soldier speaking.

"I had a strange dream last night," he was saying. "A huge cake of barley bread dropped down out of the sky and fell on one of our tents with such force that it flattened the tent to the ground. What do you think that means?"

"Think! I *know* what it means!" another voice answered. "It's a bad omen—it signifies disaster. That barley bread represents the sword of Gideon, and the destruction of the tent means our defeat."

Gideon and his servant didn't linger. Elated by what they had heard, they made haste back to their camp, where Gideon at once prepared for battle. His simple homespun scheme is one of the most familiar tales in the Old Testament. He had had no experience in military strategy, but his conduct of the battle was brilliant. It may have been the first example of psychological warfare. Real weapons were too scarce to be counted on, so he had to do without, but there were plenty of trumpets and pitchers and lamps. He divided his men into three companies of one hundred each who were to "attack" from a different position.

"Watch me," he said, "and do as I do. When I blow on my trumpet, you blow a loud blast on yours, and cry at the top of your voices, 'The sword of the Lord and of Gideon!' Then break your pitchers and take your lamps in your left hand, and with your trumpets in your right, keep blowing!"

It all happened exactly as planned. The sleeping Midianites were taken by surprise and completely demoralized. "And all the host ran, and cried, and fled." The little army of three hundred chased them clear out of the valley.

"And the country was in quietness forty years." That was quite a nice spell of peace in those days.

Gideon settled down to farming again, with a number of wives, and raised seventy children along with this crops.

He was not a great religious figure, as, for instance, Abraham was—the "friend of God." Between Gideon and God there was more of an adversary relationship. He was a folk hero, a simple man of the people, and he seems a strange choice for a great military undertaking. But somehow God can transform anyone who heeds his call so that he (or she) becomes the very one for the task. And then, by the same divine magic, he also makes the task become an inspiring opportunity.

The one real touch of idealism in Gideon's nature was his refusal of the crown, which the men of Israel, at the height of their elation and gratitude, would have given him, with the promise that his son and grandson would succeed him on the throne. To found a dynasty was a very tempting proposition. But with admirable firmness he put it from him.

"Neither I nor my son shall rule Israel, for the Lord is our ruler," he said.

So the tradition, established by Moses, that the children of Israel were a theocracy, was not broken.

Never again was Gideon called upon for military service to his country, but he had made his contribution to history, and history never forgets.

Chapter 10

A Woman Who Kept Faith with God

Hannah

In a village in the beautiful hill country of Ephraim lived a prosperous gentleman named Elkanah with his family, which consisted of two wives and several children.

From a material point of view, all the ingredients for a happy home seemed to be present. They lived well, there was no pinch of poverty. He was able each year to take his family to Shiloh for the Passover celebration, thus combining a holiday excursion with a religious observance, for they would make their sacrifices to the Lord in the tabernacle there.

But Elkanah's home was not happy, and the reason was the two wives.

Was there ever a happy home with two wives in it, I wonder? I doubt it, for it's contrary to God's plan and, therefore, against nature. In the beginning, according to the Jews' own story, God made one man and one woman, and gave them the task of peopling the earth. It was the descendants of this man, Adam, who decided they could people their share of the earth better, or at least more quickly, if they had several wives. So polygamy was established—by man, not God. It lasted for centuries but was finally abandoned before the Christian era.

In Elkanah's household, the situation was aggravated by the fact that one wife, Peninah, had all the children; the other, Hannah, none. Since Hebrew women found fulfillment only in motherhood, Hannah's humiliation was great; but Peninah made it almost insupportable, for she had no comfort or sympathy to offer. Rather she gloated over Hannah's condition and reveled in her own success. She often alluded in mean little ways to Hannah's failure to "do her duty" and called attention to her own sturdy offspring. She even hinted that Hannah must have displeased Jehovah in some way and suggested piously that Hannah search her conscience until she found the answer.

Believing that she was not guilty of any secret sin, poor Hannah suffered in silence but resented Peninah intensely. If she had only realized it, she might have felt sorry for Peninah, for Peninah, too, was an unhappy woman. Her assumption of superiority was actually pretense, for she knew that Elkanah did not love her as he loved Hannah. Of all unjust things! (she thought). Here she was, a woman who had satisfied her husband with a brood of healthy children, and he was so unappreciative and so lacking in good sense that he continually showed his preference for a weakling who was not nearly as well-favored as herself! Elkanah needn't think he was keeping his foolish infatuation a secret, either. She had heard him talking to Hannah, comforting her when he should have been blaming her. She had overheard him say tenderly, "Why do you let this grieve you so much? Am I not more to you than ten sons?" Poor Peninah! She was to be pitied, too, for it was not entirely her fault that she had to take second place. It was a deplorable situation.

That was the way things stood when the time came around for their annual journey. One day during their stay in Shiloh, Hannah slipped out and went to the tabernacle alone. For weeks she had been planning to take her problem to the place where she had been taught to feel that God was and hoping for relief for her burdened heart.

As she knelt at the altar praying and crying—for her heart was so full she could not keep back the tears—the old priest, Eli, noticed her. Though prayers were usually audible, she was making no sound. Seeing her lips moving, he thought she was babbling to herself and jumped to the conclusion that she had been drinking. That was a strange mistake for a priest to make! Perhaps his two wayward sons gave him a low opinion of human nature. This accusation shocked poor Hannah, who was already troubled. She exclaimed, "Oh, no, my lord! I am a woman with a sorrowful spirit. I have had no strong drink nor even any wine. I have been pouring out my soul to the Lord."

Then Eli answered, "Go in peace, and the God of Israel grant thee the petition that thou hast asked of him."

Hannah went away happier than she had been for a long time. She took the priest's words for a promise, not just a pious hope. She did not realize that poor ineffectual Eli had no more power to perform a miracle by by-passing the laws of nature any more than she did herself. In fact, she had far more to do with the happy outcome than he did. For her nerves relaxed, her tensions drained away, her heart was at ease. Peninah no longer had the power to hurt her. In access of expectant optimism, she returned with Elkanah to Ephraim. In that happy and healthy condition she could hardly have helped having a baby!

Sure enough, in the fullness of time, Hannah bore a son, and she called his name Samuel, "Because I have asked him of the Lord." Elkanah smiled approvingly when she told him the name she had chosen. He liked the name and its meaning.

So the God whom Hannah had thought was responsible for her childlessness was the one who sent her comfort, through his old priest. Just as Abraham, through a searing personal experience, arrived at a sublime truth about God, perhaps Hannah came to realize that God would not punish her small sins with an affliction out of all proportion to her faults, and that just as Elkanah had soothed her hurts with his sympathetic tenderness, God, being so much greater than the most loving husband, cared even more greatly. It is self-evident that later, when she became a mother, she was able to lay hold of a small portion of a God-like love.

It is at this point that Hannah becomes remarkable. Up to now she had been an ordinary women in an ordinary situation.

Ordinary for those times, that is. She *became* the Woman Who Kept Faith with God. For Hannah had made a promise at the altar that day when she had poured out her soul to the Lord. "If you will give me a son," she prayed, "I will give him back to you. All the days of his life, he shall belong to the Lord."

Though made in a whisper with trembling lips and unheard by any human ears, this to Hannah was a sacred vow. To be able to sustain a fine impulse, a high mood, a commitment is great. That is not so ordinary. Many vows and promises have been made to God when trouble threatened that were never redeemed when the danger passed. An old psalmist wrote, "I will go into thy house with burnt offerings. I will pay thee my vows which my lips have uttered and my mouth hath spoken when I was in trouble" (Ps 66:13-14). That is what Hannah did.

Something I once read tried to make her out a preternaturally wise, far-seeing, heroic woman, who had no selfish motive: "The need of the hour was for a man of God who would stir up new and prodigious forces in the depressed people of Israel, and get them back on the right track," and Hannah wanted a son to dedicate to this purpose. Some students of the Bible always try to make out that the people were super human. I think her plea *was* selfish but not unworthy. The facts show that Hannah was heroic enough for anyone, a gentle, loving woman who suffered much, finally had a little child, allowed herself to keep him a few short years where she could rock, cuddle, play with, and enjoy him; then relentlessly she let him go into the care of an old man. How could she do it? Because she was Hannah, she thought it was God's will, and she had promised him. It has been said that physical strength is measured by what one can carry, spiritual strength by what one can bear. So Hannah met the test of greatness.

What about the little boy who was lent to the Lord? What effect did this self-denial of his mother's have on him? A commentator objected to the word "lent"—said "given" would be better. But I like it. It suggests joint ownership—that the parents still had some responsibility. What better relationship could there be than for parents to share this responsibility with God?

Nobody knows just how old Samuel was when Hannah and Elkanah left him, but he was probably six or seven, old enough to help Eli. The tasks must have been small and menial those first years, but he was being taught the work of the priesthood from the ground up.

A little boy in kindergarten was fascinated on his first day by the small size of the furniture. The teacher saw him trying the chairs, sizing up the little tables, measuring the hooks that were on the wall for little coats and caps. Finally she said, "Well, Bobby, what do you think?"

His answer surprised her. "I don't like it. There's nothing to grow up to." Children are sometimes amazing.

Nothing was adjusted for Samuel. He began on the first day to grow up to a man's job. And not an ordinary man's job, either. It was to be the role of hero and saint, and Samuel eventually filled it.

Although six or seven years is not long, there was time for his character to be set in its destined mold by a mother who must have taught him from babyhood that he was to be "lent to the Lord." He grew as naturally as Jesus did, "in wisdom and stature, and in favor with God and man." If Eli or his wife had had such wisdom and devotion, what a difference it would have made in the character of their sons! Eli was not forceful enough to deal with his strong-willed wayward boys, but in Samuel he had a different proposition. I believe they may have had rapport from the first.

Although I don't think Hannah's mind was on the political situation or the future of Israel, for there is no evidence of it, I do believe she may have had a great ambition to make a big contribution to life through her son, with God's help. We have these words from an anonymous writer, "He who would accomplish little need sacrifice little; he who would achieve much must sacrifice much; he who would attain highly must sacrifice greatly." Hannah may have known and been sustained by the knowledge that as she was making a tremendous sacrifice, the results would be in proportion. She gave to Israel one of its great spiritual leaders, the first of the priestly prophets, one who had the wisdom and strength to put the whole national life on a higher level.

As we can't measure Hannah's aching loneliness and longing for her little boy that must have possessed her at times, neither can we measure the compensating pride and joy she had in her great son. But no one who lends to the Lord receives less than she gives. She had only one child, but she dreamed greatly and sacrificed much, and her harvest was commensurate.

Chapter 11

A Pastoral Romance

Ruth

The sumptuous dinner was over. The gentlemen in their elegant satins and laces had rejoined the no-less-gorgeously gowned ladies in the glittering candle-lit salon in a private home in Paris. The ambassador from the United States alone was in sober hue, wearing his accustomed brown velvet, his hair unpowdered. But Mr. Benjamin Franklin was a privileged character, and although he made no effort to ape the gay plumage of the French court, he was very popular.

The conversation at dinner had turned on the short story, and when the guests had settled themselves comfortably, Mr. Franklin drew from his pocket a manuscript.

"I have here," he said, "a little story which I have greatly enjoyed."

He wanted their opinion of it and read it aloud. All were entranced. The beauty of style, they said, the charm of the leading character, the skill displayed in developing the theme—all made a potent appeal.

"Where did you get it?" they asked. "Who wrote it?"

Franklin gravely told them it was the story of *Ruth*, and was found in the Bible. The gay Parisians of that day were not noted for their familiarity with the scriptures, and he had brought them something that to them seemed entirely new and fresh.

He could not tell them the name of the author, for it is unknown. Some things about him are known but are important only as they explain the book. It was written about one hundred years after the return of the Israelites from captivity. Its place in the Bible, following the book of *Judges*, is due to the fact that the events in the story belong to that period. The author so states in the beginning, "In the time when the judges ruled, there was a famine in the land." Several times he explains acts of his characters with the words, "This was the custom in ancient times in Israel," and at the last he mentions David, who, of course, lived in a much later period.

Another thing known from internal evidence is that the writer had a purpose, for it is a story with a message.

When the first Hebrew exiles were allowed by King Cyrus of Persia to return to Judah, they found that the remnant of the population that had been left behind had intermarried with their neighbors—Samaritans, Moabites, or anyone at all. This was considered by some an appalling situation, for the Hebrews' ideal from earliest times had been a pure blood line. This meant no fraternizing with "heathens." But to others it was not so bad. They may have taken the more realistic view that it was all that had saved from extinction those who remained. At any rate, the number of mixed marriages had begun to increase.

To Nehemiah, the governor, and Ezra, the priest, this was the same as apostasy—renouncing of the faith—and they instituted some drastic reforms. Using the power of their offices, they began going into homes, exiling the foreign wives and husbands, and punishing the Israelites. Their methods were inhumane and cruel, and much suffering resulted. With the government and the church on the same side, there was no one to appeal to, no one to speak for the people and their homes.

Then a little book appeared. It may have been written anonymously and circulated secretly. In the cleverest way possible, the author got in on the blind side of the reader by making his charming young heroine not a Hebrew maiden but a Moabite girl. He played down the differences in the two peoples and wrote of intermarriage simply, without apology, as if it were perfectly natural. He implied that true love was not a matter of race. He hinted that God is no respecter of persons. Then at the last, he delivered a broadside against bigotry by saying, "Of course, this was the girl who became the great-grandmother of our beloved King David." He must have chuckled over that as he wrote it, for if Ruth had polluted that blood line, it was a taint many a family would have been glad to have!

So we see that the author was a liberal of his time, with ideas at variance with the narrow, chauvinistic ones supported by both governor and priest, and the story he wrote was probably the first ever written dealing with the race problem! It has survived for other reasons, just as *Gulliver's Travels*, written by Swift as a satire, has survived as an adventure story. Since Ruth is a real character, there may have been a legend about her which the author took and developed with his imagination, as if someone should make a long story out of the cherry tree incident, and so it becomes an historical romance.

Mary Ellen Chase, and other writers about the Bible, place this story with the books of literature of the Old Testament. It was not a folk-tale, passed along orally, growing and changing with repetition, for it is too perfect in form. It was the work of one mind only.

The story has a good beginning. In the first verse the author gives the situation and introduces the characters, and then he starts the action.

"Now it happened, in the days when the judges ruled, that there was a famine in the land."

Living in Bethlehem in the drought-stricken land of Judah was a man named Elimelech. He and his wife, Naomi, decided that the situation would be bad for some time to come, and the only way to feed their growing boys was to move. They decided on Moab, a neighboring country, where they had reason to believe Elimelech could make a living.

It was the same situation as in the United States in the 1930s during the Great Depression when many businesses, especially in the south, closed; houses had to be given up, and people moved away. All of the families I knew expected to return, and some did, but most did not. Probably Elimelech expected to go back, expected to bring up his boys in Bethlehem. But moves are hard to make, and before he had accomplished it, death put a final period to his life.

After that, it was impossible for Naomi. It was all she could do to keep the wolf from the door, as she brought up her sons, Mahlon and Chilion, alone. They must have liked their playmates in Moab when they were children, and when they reached man's estate, they quite naturally fell in love with two attractive Moabite girls. Their names were Ruth and Orpah.

Then followed what must have been happy years. There were four for Naomi to love and care for, two families under her hospitable roof. But another blow fell. With the stark simplicity of the Bible, unsoftened by detail or explanation, the story says the sons died. Both together? How? Was it an accident? But by his indifference to any curiosity in his readers, the author is showing that these deaths are unimportant except as they advance the plot. Mahlon and Chilion have to be eliminated in the interest of this story.

After the last funeral, when the freshness of their grief was dulled a little, the three who were left talked things over. There was now no reason for Naomi to remain away from her relatives and her old home. The girls would return to the homes they had left when they married, and in time they would be sought by other men.

"I pray that the Lord will deal kindly with you," she said to them, "as you have both dealt kindly with our dead, and with me."

This was to be another sad parting, for the girls loved Naomi, who had always "dealt kindly" with them. But they knew there was no better plan than the one she suggested. When she had packed what she could carry of her personal belongings and was ready to start, on foot, to Bethlehem, Ruth and Orpah said they would walk with her a part of the way. Naomi was touched and grateful. But when they reached the border, she stopped and said, "You mustn't come any farther. . . . It's a long way back."

As she held out her arms to her two daughters-in-law, tears began to roll down her cheeks. There was a sad little scene at the roadside as the three women, all weeping, held to each other. Then, in order to make them smile, I think, for a smile is the quickest way to dry tears, she referred jokingly to the custom of one brother marrying the widow of another.

"There's not a chance Mahlon and Chilion will have any brothers! I'm not likely to have another husband, and even if I did, and had sons, would you want to wait for them to grow up?"

But her feeble joke only made them cry harder. Finally Orpah, obedient to her insistence, kissed Naomi again and started back, saying, "Come on, Ruth." But Ruth clung to Naomi and uttered some of the most moving lines in all literature: "Entreat me not to leave thee, or to return from following after thee. For whither thou goest, I will go, and where thou lodgest I will lodge. Thy people shall be my people, and thy God my God. Where thou diest will I die, and there will I be buried. The Lord do so to me and more also, if aught but death part thee and me."

This first part of the story is Naomi's. Although Ruth now moves into the spotlight and the action centers around her, and the romance is hers, the story might as fittingly have been named *Naomi*. For it was the older woman who set in motion the train of circumstances that were responsible for what happened in Bethlehem.

Naomi wouldn't have been human if she had not dreamed about this homecoming—seeing the old home, the loved spots of her young womanhood, and especially the old friends—and she wouldn't have been a typical woman if she hadn't hoped they might say, "How well you look! Moab certainly agreed with you—you look younger than when you went away." It would be a kindly fiction, she knew, meaning she looked good to them.

But this did not happen. She had been away too long. Too many years had passed; she had experienced too many griefs. Her hair was white now. The gap she and her family had left had long since been filled. Her friends said to each other, "Is this Naomi? How she has changed!"

The more tactless said to her, "I would never have known you."

Naomi's answer shows her hurt. "Don't call me Naomi. Just call me 'Mara,' for the Almighty hath dealt very bitterly with me."

The author closed the chapter with a line that sounds unimportant—"And they came to Bethlehem in the beginning of barley harvest"—but which had a great bearing on the events that followed.

A place to live seems to have been no problem for Naomi. Elimelech had probably owned a house. Maybe a relative had been living in it and kept it in good condition. But they had to have food, and as Naomi was on her home ground, and she was the older woman, it was up to her to have an idea. And she had one. She impresses me as a person who would never sit down and starve for lack of an idea. The author skips something here, because it would have been well-known to his readers; but Naomi would have explained her plan, perhaps in this wise: "We have a law by which women in our situation are taken care of, as far as grain is concerned. We are allowed to glean after the reapers in the fields."

The law was stated like this: "When thou cuttest thy harvest and hast forgot a sheaf in the field, thou shalt not go again to fetch it—it shall be for the stranger, for the fatherless, and for the widow." That was part of Judea's provision for the poor.

Probably some people complained at being compelled to share anything, and some because they had to go and gather for themselves, for in every age and in every economic stratum there are those who grumble.

When Naomi had explained this custom to Ruth, Ruth said, "Let me be the one to go." Perhaps she added, "I'm the younger and stronger, and I like being outdoors. It will be fun."

Naomi answered, "Go, my daughter."

Now it was Ruth's "hap" to go to a part of the field owned by Boaz, a rich landowner who lived in the town and had an overseer to operate the farm, a custom not peculiar to Judea. It also "happed" that Boaz went to the farm that day.

When he arrived, he said to the reapers, "The Lord be with you," and they answered, "The Lord bless thee."

What a nice man! He treated his hired hands as if they were people, with feelings, not just automatons who lived for nothing but to serve him.

After a while he noticed Ruth and liked what he saw. It may have been a sweet face, a modest demeanor, grace of movement— or all of these. He said to his overseer, "Who is that?"

The other answered, "That is a Moabitish damsel who came back with Naomi. She came up to me this morning and said politely, 'I pray thee, may I have your permission to gather after the reapers?' And I said, 'Sure; go ahead.' So she went to work and has been at it all day."

More light is shed on Boaz' character by the overseer's confidence that the boss would approve what he had done, even though it involved not a Jewish maiden but an alien. (It is not unusual for employees to take on the coloration of their employers, for good or ill!)

After watching her awhile, Boaz went to Ruth, probably told her who he was, and then said, "I suggest you stay here and glean in my field all through barley harvest. You will be treated well. I have spoken to my men about you, and they will not bother you, and you will find plenty to glean. When you are thirsty, feel free to drink of the vessels that are kept full of fresh water for my men."

It is very likely that many men in Boaz' position tried to discourage the poor from coming and didn't allow them a thing more than the law required. They would justify this by saying, "You just have to make it unpleasant for those people. Give 'em an inch and they'll take a mile. Make it pleasant for them, and they'd swarm all over your land."

Ruth may have been prepared for some coldness and discourtesy, which would explain why Boaz' kindness nearly overcame her. She may also have been aware of the fact that the Hebrews were an exclusive people, who didn't make things easy for aliens, and so in her surprise and gratitude she bowed nearly to the ground.

"Why are you so kind to me, a stranger?" she asked humbly.

Boaz answered, "Your story is known to me—how you chose, after the death of your husband, to leave your kindred and the land of your nativity and to come with your mother-in-law to her country and her people. May the Lord God of Israel, under whose wings you have come to trust, reward you with peace and happiness."

Sincere gratitude often has the effect of making people do even more than they intended. Maybe that is why Boaz went on, "At mealtime, you join my men, and there will be bread for you, and parched corn, and vinegar for you to dip your morsels in."

Vinegar and parched corn! What a menu! I can't imagine what the women were thinking of to send the men off to work with that in their lunch pails. One Bible commentator said of the vinegar,

"It's very refreshing," but I noticed he did not say, "Try it sometime." Perhaps, along with the parched corn the men needed something with more authority than water.

The more Boaz saw of Ruth, the better he liked her. During the afternoon he said to his reapers, "Let her glean even among the sheaves, and drop some handfuls on purpose now and then, where she is gathering."

So Ruth gleaned until evening, and when she had beaten the grain out of the husks she found, she had a whole ephah of barley! That was more than she had dared hope for. She hurried home to tell Naomi of her strange day. I can imagine Naomi's eyes sparkling as she saw the size of the sack.

"Where did you glean today to get all that?"

"It was the field of a man named Boaz."

Naomi was really excited then. "Boaz! Why, he's our near kinsman. This is wonderful!"

This emotion was catching. Ruth thought of something else to add to Naomi's delight. "He told me to come to his field every day and follow his young men until the end of the harvesting."

This meant that they had security until winter. It worked out even better than they knew at the time, for wheat harvest followed, and there was still work, always seasoned with courtesy and kindness, in Boaz' field. So the fall passed, and winter came.

It was during the winter that Naomi decided that Boaz, a bachelor, would be an ideal husband for Ruth.

Now at this point the author made use of a quaint old custom in vogue at that time. As he did not explain it, it must have been generally understood. It was certainly quaint! So quaint it's no wonder it faded out. It was the parents' place to arrange marriages, and Naomi stood in that place toward Ruth. The young women had complete confidence in the older, so when her mother-in-law unfolded her plan for a second marriage for Ruth, Ruth obeyed unquestioningly.

"Boaz will be winnowing barley tonight in the threshing room," said Naomi, "and will sleep there. When he has finished and has eaten his supper and lain down to sleep, go quietly, uncover his feet and lie down there, and when he wakes he will tell you what to do."

Boaz woke up about midnight and was turning over, when he saw a woman lying at his feet.

He was startled and exclaimed, "Who are you?"

"I am Ruth," she answered timidly, "and I have come here because you are a near kinsman."

Being a modest man, Boaz was delighted at this sign that Ruth had turned to him instead of waiting for offers from younger men. Her sweetness and grace had not gone unnoticed. "Don't be afraid," he said. "I will do all that is needful, for you are admired throughout my city as a young woman of character."

And so they were married. In due course a little son was born, whom they called Obed, "and Naomi became nurse unto it."

All who are grandmothers will understand Naomi's delight as she started loving and cherishing a new generation. The neighbors, too, rejoiced with the family. They had long since gotten over their stiffness, and they had come to love Ruth. Everyone was happy about the whole thing, and they were glad the first one was a boy. They said to Naomi, "You are fortunate. You have a fine daughter-in-law who loves you and is better to you than seven sons!"

That was high praise, particularly for a foreign daughter-in-law. Then in a quiet but effective way, the author points out in conclusion that Ruth, the girl of alien blood, became the great-grandmother of their most beloved king, David.

The author has carried out his purpose—to combat the point of view that intermarriage was a very bad thing—in a delightful way. The story illustrated beautifully the fact that knowing people helps us to understand them, and understanding helps us to like them. The old saying,"Familiarity breeds contempt," is true only when a thing is contemptible. Familiarity may breed a long list of delightful things: friendship, understanding, sympathy, appreciation, love.

The other characters in the story do credit to the Jewish people. Boaz is a perfect example of a gentleman, kind to his employees, as courteous to a girl in the field as to a lady in his drawing room. One knows that Ruth will have a happy home. Then there's Naomi, brave, wise, good, and kind. There is no doubt that she had been one of the finest influences in the lives of Ruth and Orpah. She was an ideal representative of her religion, and she had a superior religion. She had brought up her sons in the traditions of their country and faith, to honor their mothers as well as their fathers, to protect the poor and weak, to be clean in their private lives. No heathen religion taught such things. This little home on foreign soil must have been a bit of heaven to the two Moabitish girls. Orpah, too, appreciated and admired its spirit, but Ruth clave to it.

These three women are interesting examples of three types. Naomi is the woman who demonstrates in her life the elements of her faith and does it so well she becomes an unconscious influence, drawing others to her belief. Orpah is an example of those who may see and admire but do not act; she dropped back into the old life. Ruth is an example of those who see the best, recognize it, covet it, and cleave to it. She responded by joining her life and influence to Naomi's, and the two became a foundation on which God could build something wonderful, and he did.

As for the author—the unknown person who so many, many years ago held the ideal of brotherhood and made it the heart of a gentle romance—his influence is still alive, still reminding us that God is the Father of all and that true worship is translated into love for our brethren.

Chapter 12

The Courageous Queen

Esther

There are in the Bible two books (and only two) named for women. Both are historical romances, both are by unknown authors, but in spirit they are worlds apart. They were written by persons who were as different in their ideals and purposes as people can be, yet both were Jews.

Ruth was written to condemn racial intolerance; *Esther* to exalt nationalism and inspire hatred for the Jews' enemies. *Ruth* was about simple, natural people in familiar rural scenes. Good people; there was no villain at all—a story without a single bad guy. We have no trouble identifying with Ruth or Naomi, assuming that we could act with the same grace, charm, and wisdom.

But only by the wildest stretch of the imagination can we feature ourselves as anyone in the book of *Esther*, where there is a stupid king, a double-dyed villain, and a lot of silly courtiers. While Esther and Mordecai are superb, the setting and situation are like a nightmare from the *Arabian Nights*, in which the author indulged himself with a lot of fantastic details.

Many people have thought this book should not be in the Bible at all, because of the violence and blood-letting and the fact that God is not mentioned. But these objections can be easily disposed of (it seems to me). God is referred to indirectly, and his presence and interest are implied. The Jews' belief in the certainty of his punishment of their enemies, who were also *his* enemies, is a very real force in the story. Jesus told many stories where the name of

God was not mentioned. They were secular stories, but they taught religious truths. The author of *Esther* was saying, through the medium of a secular story, to the Jews of about 165 B.C., "Don't lose heart. God is still with us. He cares what happens to us. He will deliver us." It did accomplish its purpose of strengthening the morale and bolstering the courage of the Jews at a time when they were victims of cruel persecutions ordered by Antiochus Epiphanes, King of Syria. Their retaliation, when they got an opportunity to avenge themselves, was just as ruthless, for they knew nothing about forgiving their enemies; but unlike the Gentiles they took no spoils.

This story, which is based on history, is at least a footnote in the long struggle of the Jewish people and deserves a place in the record.

The name of the king in the story is Ahasuerus, but the inspiration for this character was Xerxes, who ruled Persia in the third century B.C. Ahasuerus shows up as merely stupid and compassionless, but Xerxes was an absolute monarch of unbridled cruelty. Let's draw on history for a snapshot profile of him before moving on to the story. He once started out to conquer Greece. He assembled the greatest army the world had ever seen—two million fighting men, and so many slaves and servants that the total was nearer ten million. They had to cross the Hellespont, and so two pontoon bridges had been built. But a bad storm came up and destroyed both bridges. Xerxes was so furious he had the engineers brought and beheaded. Not satisfied with that, he had the waves lashed with whips and chains thrown across the strait to show he was master! Other engineers were then conscripted and set to work on new bridges. Poor fellows! They must have quaked in their boots.

When at last the army was ready to move, Xerxes, after reviewing it, remarked, "I weep at the thought that one hundred years hence this fine army will be a bunch of moldering bones." He was much too optimistic—it lasted hardly any time. First to cross was his "sacred chariot," drawn by eight white horses and guarded by the king's bodyguard, who were called "The Immortals"—more wishful thinking. Next the foot soldiers; it took a week for them to cross. They were followed by chariots equipped with scythes on the wheels. Last came the baggage wagons. There were so many of them it took them a month to cross. They were carrying such things as costly hangings for officers' tents, soft couches, and solid gold dishes. This is history, remember—not fiction, nor my imagination.

In Thessaly, between mountains and sea, is the famous pass of Thermopylae, or Hot Gateway, through which they had to go to reach Greece. It was named in the days when "hot" referred only to heat, and was due to warm springs near by. The pass was guarded by a small body of men under a Spartan king. All the world knows his name was Leonidas. Xerxes sent him word to direct his men to surrender their arms. To his surprise, Leonidas' answer was, "Come and take them." To his still greater surprise, he found he could not, even with all his mighty host, for he could get only a few soldiers at a time into the pass. He would have had to make a humiliating return (it was a pity for him he did not!), but he found a moral loophole, a Greek traitor, who for a handful of coins showed the enemy of his country a way over the mountains. So they marched on to Athens and burned the city.

A naval battle was next on the program. Where or how Xerxes got boats, I don't know. He had a throne built for himself on a mountain and sat there to watch the fun. But the fun was spoiled when the Greeks defeated him soundly. That was the battle of Salamis, and Xerxes in a fit of childish petulance returned to Persia, leaving the war to his generals. There were two more battles, in both of which the Greeks were victorious. Only a small part of the Persian army was left to escape, leaving the slaves and the baggage behind. So the Greeks got all that gold table service and the fancy hangings to pay for their trouble! It did not pay for their losses, though.

So this cruel and capricious despot, with the mind of a child, was the real-life prototype of the king whom the beautiful Jewish girl in the fictional romance married. It was after this disastrous campaign that the events of the book are supposed to have occurred.

Let us now return to the story.

The place is Sushan, the palace(mentioned in Neh 1:1), in a city in Persia, and the time is the third year of the reign of King

Ahasuerus. In that year he made a great feast to which all the lords and nobles of the city and the provinces were invited. This "feast" lasted for six months, for the king's purpose was to show off "the riches of his glorious kingdom and the honor of his excellent majesty." (Now the author must have known as well as we do that that was fantastic to the point of being incredible, so I suggest that it was dripping with irony. You will notice other details in the story that, like our fairy tales, are not expected to be taken literally.)

This affair was such a success that when it was over the king entertained again, this time with a small party for all those who lived within the palace. This was held in the garden court and lasted a week. The wine was served in gold cups, no two of which were alike. No women were invited to the king's party, so the queen, Vashti, gave a feast for them in her apartments.

On the seventh day, when the king was "merry with wine," or, more accurately, when he was so drunk he no longer cared for decency or had any respect for the queen, he summoned Vashti to come and let the drunken courtiers see how beautiful she was.

Even by their own standards, this was a dreadful thing to do. She sent back word that he was crazy and she wasn't coming. This defiance was taking her life in her hand, for it was not a time or a situation when a defied husband could do nothing but argue. This oriental king could and did.

However, he never originated any ideas himself. He always had to ask someone. So he turned to his "wise men" and demanded, "What shall we do unto the queen Vashti according to law because she has flouted the king's command?"

I don't think he was too much concerned about the law, for he had those wise men whose special duty it was to humor each crazy or cruel whim of the monarch. So now, one of them, speaking for all, said sonorously, "Queen Vashti has not only done wrong to the king, but to all husbands in the realm. For when the shocking news gets out—as it will—that the queen has defied her husband the king, all women will be emboldened to do likewise. So an example must be made of Queen Vashti.

"If it please the king, let it be written in the laws of the Medes and Persians that Vashti shall be removed from her royal estate and it be given to another. And when that news is spread throughout the empire, all our wives will get the message."

This pronouncement pleased the king, and it was carried out without delay.

When the king's anger had cooled, that is to say when he was sober enough to realize what he had done and to be sorry for it, he might even have had the thought of venting his feelings on some of his courtiers. So they lost no time coming up with a fresh idea to distract their erratic monarch.

"Let's have a beauty contest, with the king as sole judge," they said. "We can send messengers to all the provinces to say the king wants the fairest maidens to be brought to Shushan the palace, where they will be in the women's quarters in the care of the chamberlain until the king has chosen one of them to be his new queen."

The king was delighted with this suggestion, and poor Vashti was forgotten.

Now there was living in Shushan a Jew who had been carried away from Jerusalem with the captives taken by Nebuchadnezzar. Years had passed, and no one remembered that he was a Jew. He was an intelligent and capable man who had risen to a position of importance and lived in the palace. Living in his care was a young cousin whom he had taken charge of on the death of her parents. Her name was Hadassah, but the people in Shushan had given her a nickname, Ishtar, which meant star, for she was very beautiful, and that was the name of the Persian goddess of beauty. (Esther is the Hebrew version). So of course she was included among the girls who were assembled in the house of the women to await her appearance before the king.

It came to pass that the king loved Esther above all the women, and she obtained grace and favor in his sight, so that he set the royal crown upon her head and made her queen instead of Vashti.

By a lucky chance, soon afterwards, Mordecai overheard two men plotting against the king. He told Esther, who reported it to the king. The men were found guilty, and the affair was recorded in the court chronicles. Although no notice was taken of Mordecai's involvement then, the time came when it helped him greatly.

Now Ahasuerus had a favorite courtier, just such a man as he himself was, which should occasion no surprise. His name was Haman. Although a commoner, he had been elevated to a position above all the princes and other courtiers, and the king had commanded that all were to bow in the same reverential way to him that they did to the king. The other courtiers may not have liked this very much, but they did it. All, that is, except Mordecai. He had too much self-respect to abase himself before a man he knew to be a particularly shoddy piece of humanity, and to whom he owed no loyalty.

Being an upstart with an inferiority complex, Haman could not bear an affront to his pride, so he set out to avenge himself on Mordecai. I believe he hired spies to ferret out everything they could, for they learned that he was a Jew. That was ammunition enough! So Haman hatched a diabolical scheme—he would get rid not only of Mordecai, but of all the Jews in Persia at one clever stroke. He went to the king with a bunch of lies and half-truths. He said the Jews were a dispersed people, living throughout the kingdom. That was true. He said, "They have their own laws." That was half true—they had never been completely assimilated, and never would be. He said, "They don't keep our laws." That was untrue. He said, "They are an unprofitable people." That was untrue; they paid taxes, and Haman indirectly conceded this when he said he would pay ten thousand talents of silver into the treasury to compensate the king for the revenues he would lose if he would empower Haman to get rid of them. It's my opinion that he counted on the king's refusing this gesture, and in a sense he did. He told Haman to use the silver toward the expenses of the pogrom.

"And the king took his ring from his hand and gave it unto Haman, the Jews' enemy."

The king's scribes were set to work, and letters in the name of the king and sealed with his ring were sent to all the provinces, telling the governors that on the 13th day of Adar all the Jews were to be killed, young and old, little children and women. It was all to be done in one day, and all their possessions taken as spoils. The posts went out at top speed.

"And the king and Haman sat down to drink."

A heartless picture. They cared nothing for the cruelty, blood-shed, and suffering that would ensue.

"But the city of Shushan was perplexed." There must have been decent people among the Persians who asked, "What is their crime? What have they done?"

As soon as this horrible command reached the provinces, a cry went up to heaven from the Jews. They fasted as they mourned and prayed, but there was nothing they could do but watch the day of massacre creep up. The country became a huge death cell from which there was no escape.

Esther hadn't been told, but she heard that Mordecai was sitting at the king's gate in sackcloth and ashes, which were signs of deep mourning, so she sent her chamberlain to learn the cause. And Mordecai told the whole story, including Haman's involvement, not omitting the ten thousand talents, and also sent a copy of the king's letter.

Then Mordecai said, "Tell her she must go to the king to beg for the lives of her people."

The chamberlain came back with Esther's answer.

"I *can't* do that. You know the law. It might cost me my life. And I'm out of favor just now. The king hasn't sent for me for thirty days."

I know Mordecai must have loved this girl he had reared, and dreaded to put her in such danger, but it shows the desperate urgency of the matter when he sent word, "You must take the risk. You and I would not be spared, for we are both Jews, and there is no one else to speak for our people. Besides, who knows but that you have come to the kingdom for such a time as this?"

Then Esther sent her pathetic last message to her cousin. "Gather together all the Jews in the city and fast for me three days. I, also, and my maidens will fast. Then I will go in unto the king, which is against the law, and if I perish, I perish."

Fasting was always accompanied by prayer and was proof of religious faith. If only for this one scene, I consider this a religious book, for Esther was going to perform a religious act—an act of love—the greatest act possible to a human being. She was going to offer her life for her friends.

During those three days, Esther found the strength to do what she had to do. Courage was not all she needed. It was not enough just to go impetuously in to the king, letting the deliverance of her people depend on the king's mood of the moment. It was imperative that she should not fail. So she used her head. She decided that she would not blurt out her real purpose; she must not jeopardize everything by proceeding too hastily. She would begin with a simple request that she believed the king would grant, always provided she lived to state it.

So, taking her courage in her hand, she put on her royal robes and presented herself at the door of the inner court, which was the king's apartment.

Whenever I think of Esther, I see her as she was painted by W. L. Taylor long ago. She wore a dress of canary yellow and had wide arm bands that emphasized the shapeliness of her arms. Her long dark hair hung in braids over her shoulders. The fingers of her right hand were touching the wall behind her as if for support. There was an indescribable expression in her beautiful dark eyes—not fear, but an awareness of danger, a waiting expression. Perhaps I'm reading something into it that was not there—it was so long ago—but that is the picture that presents itself to my mind's eye.

She found favor with the king! He too liked the picture she made, and he extended his scepter, and she drew near and touched the top of it. Then said the king, "What wilt thou, Queen Esther, and what is thy request? It shall be given thee, even to the half of my kingdom."

A very extravagant promise was a cliche in those days. I wonder if anyone ever had the temerity to claim it!

Esther's relief can only be imagined. That terrible danger passed, she made her first request.

"If it seem good unto the king, let the king and Haman come today to the banquet I have prepared for him."

He accepted with pleasure and sent word to Haman to make hast and present himself at the palace, for they were going to dine with the queen. So they went. I am sure Esther spared no trouble or expense to make it lovely, the food good and plentiful, and herself a charming hostess, and the king enjoyed it.

At last he laid down his napkin, pushed back his chair, and said, "What is thy petition and it shall be granted thee. And what is thy request? Even to the half of the kingdom it shall be performed."

But Esther wasn't yet ready. A second banquet would strengthen the impressions in the king's mind. Three times would be overdoing it, but it is natural to want to repeat a good time at least once. So she said, "My request is that you and Haman come again tomorrow to the banquet that I shall prepare for you."

Again, the invitation pleased the king. Perhaps he didn't get many invitations to dinner, as not many people would care to risk their lives cultivating such a capricious and unpredictable ruler.

On the way home, Haman walked on air. He called in his wife, Zeresh, and his relatives and neighbors to hear about his honors. He was the only man invited with the king! The queen had plainly taken a fancy to him. He was going again tomorrow! Then his face clouded, and he stormed, "But it is all spoiled when I see Mordecai the Jew! When I passed him, he neither bowed nor nodded. Just looked right through me."

Zeresh came to his rescue with a comforting suggestion, "I'll tell you what! Have a great gallows built, fifty cubits high [75 feet], and tomorrow ask the king to let you hang Mordecai on it. Then you can go merrily in to the banquet with nothing on your mind."

The idea pleased Haman, and he set carpenters to work at once.

Now follows a scene of pure comedy, the best part of the story. That night the king couldn't sleep. If there is one thing I'm sure of, it is that it was not his conscience that kept him awake. My guess is that it was due to too much rich food and no exercise. Whenever he couldn't sleep, he would wake up a chamberlain to come and read to him. The chamberlain, poor fellow, probably wasn't troubled that way at all but had to sit up with the king. There wasn't much reading matter to choose from. Very likely the only book in the palace was the court chronicles, so that is what he read. As he was droning along, he came to the item about Mordecai saving the king's life.

"Wait," Ahasuerus said to the chamberlain. "What reward did Mordecai receive for that?"

"None, sir."

Ahasuerus was surprised and wanted to remedy that oversight, but as usual he had to get an idea from someone else. So he asked, "Who is in the court?"

The chamberlain looked and reported, "Haman has just come in."

"Good. Ask him to come here."

I can't imagine why Haman was there if it was still night. Maybe it was now dawn, and he had come early because he was in a hurry to get permission to hang Mordecai.

As soon as he came in, the king said, "What shall we do for the man the king delighteth to honor?"

Here is one of the story's most delicious little ironies: the man who wanted to honor Mordecai asked the man who wanted to murder him for suggestions, and Haman was trapped and betrayed by his own self-love. He thought, "Whom but me does he want to honor? Who has been getting all the favors around here lately? It can't be anyone else."

So pretending he had no idea what was in the king's mind (and how right he was!), he said, "For the man whom the king delighteth to honor, let royal apparel which the king wears be brought,and the king's own horse, and the royal crown; and let one of the king's most noble princes array him and set him on the horse, and then lead him through the streets proclaiming to all, 'Thus shall it be done to the man whom the king delighteth to honor'."

Then the most appalling words that ever fell on Haman's ears assailed them now.

"Fine," said his majesty. "Do all that you have said to Mordecai, the Jew. Let nothing be left undone."

Haman's face must have been green, but he had to carry out the revolting charade.

And Mordecai? What were his sensations? Being human, he must have felt exactly as you or I would have.

When it was all over, Haman covered his head (in today's world he would have turned up his coat collar and pulled his hat brim down) and hurried home. Even there, as family and neighbors gathered round, he didn't get the sympathy he expected.

Were they heartily sick of his airs and arrogance? His wife said, "Oh, oh. If Mordecai is a Jew, before whom you have already begun to fall, he'll get you in the end."

This remark serves a wider purpose than just a commentary on Haman's unfeeling wife. It was a word of encouragement to the Jews who read the story. It said to them, "You will win in the end"—the inference being because they *were* Jews, the Chosen People.

The next day Haman went again to the queen's banquet, but not merrily at all. He had not, of course, mentioned to the king his own plan for disposing of Mordecai. You didn't honor a man and hang him for nothing the same day. Again Esther had done everything possible to make the evening a success, and once more the king promised to grant her petition up to the half of his kingdom. Now she was ready.

"If it please the king, let my life be given me at my petition, and my people at my request. For we are sold, I and my people, to be destroyed, to be slain, and to perish."

The king's surprise was genuine. "Who is he that durst presume in his heart to do so?"

This was the moment Esther was waiting for. Pointing her finger at Haman, she said dramatically, "There is the man, that wicked Haman!"

The favor of this king, which could veer like a weathercock in a high wind, turned against the trembling Haman. He wanted to give immediate release to his fury, but as usual had no ideas; so a chamberlain made a suggestion.

"There is a gallows fifty cubits high in Haman's house which had built for Mordecai."

Without a second's hesitation, the king said, "Hang him on it."

So they hanged Haman on the gallows he had prepared for Mordecai, and the king's wrath was appeased.

Then Mordecai was sent for and received the tremendous news that he and his people had been saved by the courage of the young queen. The king gave Haman's property to her, and she promptly gave it to Mordecai. The king even took off his ring, which he had given to Haman, and gave it to Mordecai.

This was all very wonderful, but Mordecai and Esther did not forget for a moment that their people were in danger of annihilation on 13 of Adar. So Esther made one more plea, and Ahasuerus granted it. At once new letters, countermanding Haman's order, were sent to the provinces by riders on horses, mules, camels, and young dromedaries. In other words, everything with four legs was pressed into service, so that the message reached every province in time.

I wish the writer of this story had stopped here, with forgiveness and merry-making all around. When the day came, there was a terrible slaughter, for the king's order had simply given permission to the Jews to defend themselves and fight back. Many of the Persians fought for the Jews, for now they feared Mordecai, the new favorite, and with their help 75,000 of the Jews' enemies were slain. But Mordecai was not like Haman and never would be. No spoils were taken, for he had so ordered; this was in his view a religious war, and they were not to profit by it. At his suggestion, the 14th day of Adar was established as a day of gladness and feasting and of gift-giving to each other. The idea caught on, and as time went on the anniversary became known as the Feast of Purim (because "Haman had cast Pur, that is, lots, to destroy them.")

If this story had, indeed, ended in a scene of forgiveness and peace, it would have been completely unrealistic, for at that time it could not have happened. When we consider that the official position of the church when Jesus came was still "an eye for an eye," and that their enemies were enemies of the faith and therefore God's enemies who must be exterminated, we can see why Jesus met such amazed and bitter opposition. His gentle doctrine of returning good for evil simply confounded priests and people. "*Forgive* our enemies, *pray* for those who mistreat us, *love* those who persecute us?"

"Why, yes. If you love only those who love you, what thanks have ye? Don't even publicans and sinners do that?"

Yes. They had to admit it was so.

"Then what do ye more than others?" he asked reasonably.

Was Jesus too soft? overly sentimental? thinking only of the man who had done wrong, forgetting the one who had been wronged? No, he was thinking of both. He knew the spirit of vengeance was as harmful to the one as to the other; that it is destructive to both, a bad influence in the world, increasing its unhappiness. That no one gains by it; all who practice it are victims. On the other hand, forgiveness is a constructive force, blessing not only the one who receives it, but the one who gives.

Purim is still observed by orthodox Jews, but as a happy time of feasting and gift-giving. So the Christian spirit of love and forgiveness outlasts the spirit of vengeance, and always triumphs in the end.

Chapter 13

The Reluctant Missionary

Jonah

If asked, "What do you know about Jonah?" a great many people would answer promptly, "He was swallowed by a whale" but if pressed for more would be unable to add a word.

This is a pity, because *Jonah* is one of the most brilliant books in the Old Testament.

When I was a child, it was treated as a test of orthodoxy, the implication being that one who could believe that story could believe anything and was therefore a better church member and a better Christian. Later it dwindled into a rather shop-worn joke. This failure of appreciation for the sublime message of the book was due to the attempt to have it taken literally.

It has been described as a sermon, or even as a letter, with great cleverness, to present a highly unpopular subject: God's *universal* love. Since many of the Jews of that time felt exactly as Jonah, that they were God's only people and did not want this comfortable belief challenged, the unknown author had to be very clever indeed to get read at all. That is why he did not write a conventional sermon but slipped up on their blind side, so to speak. He also laid his story in a long-past period, when the idea of evangelizing the heathen was as unthinkable as cannibalism, so that readers would not be on the defensive, feeling that their toes were being stepped on.

The date of the writing was sometime in the third or fourth century B.C., in the post-captivity period, when the Jews were back in Jerusalem and had entered into an extremely nationalistic period. Mary Ellen Chase sets the date at about 200 B.C. It follows logically, although by more than one hundred years, the book of *Ruth*, which was an attack on racial prejudice. "We must like all people for all are God's children," was the message of *Ruth*. And now comes this author saying, "We must *evangelize* all people."

Where did he get the idea for his plot? If I hadn't done a little research, I would have said, "Surely out of his own head, for there was never another like it!" But I'd have been wrong. This writer knew his own history better than I did. He must have known that the prophet Jeremiah, 200 years earlier, had written (Jer 51:34) this strange metaphor, "Nebuchadnezzar, King of Babylon, hath devoured me. He hath swallowed me up like a dragon. He hath filled his belly with my delicacies. He hath cast me out."

The analogy in that case was never in doubt—Jeremiah referred to Israel's captivity and her release. I can almost see and hear our author chuckling over the notion of using that figure, only he would change the dragon into a big fish, which would be just as fantastic a touch, but his own. He would also have his character spewed out alive.

Now for his hero (or non-hero), he drew on history again. Away back in 2 Kings 14, a man is mentioned whose name was Jonah. He was the son of Amittai, the prophet. From the brief reference, we see that the real Jonah was hand in glove with the king, Jeroboam II, "who did evil in the sight of the Lord." He did succeed in grabbing some territory for Israel, but the *Abingdon Bible Commentary* says the material gains "resulted in a most disastrous lowering of the religious and moral tone of society" and in hardships for the poor. This appraisal is based on the writings of both Amos and Hosea, who were contemporary prophets. So if the original Jonah could be called a prophet, he was far different from those whose careers have given that profession its exalted image. As a colleague and supporter of the king whose aims were material and whose methods were unscrupulous, he might be called an "Israel Firster," which is probably why our author chose him.

There is no further mention of this original Jonah until, 300 years later, a world-minded man, name unknown, wrote a story in which he figured as chief character. It's as if a writer today should make one of the soldiers who crossed the Delaware with Washington the chief character in a novel.

The story begins with God's instruction to Jonah. "Arise, go to Ninevah, that great city, and cry against it, for their wickedness is come up before me."

Ninevah did indeed merit the most severe condemnation, for its sins were shocking. Historians tell us that it was great in physical and materialistic terms; for nearly two centuries it had been the capital and the richest city of western Asia. For more than one century, it had set the fashions in clothes and art. It had most of the world's trade. Great roads converged there, and it was filled with people of all nationalities. It was famous for its temples and palaces, but the majority of the people took no pride in them, for they represented only taxation and misery. The plain people were treated cruelly by soldiers and others in power, who thought nothing of pushing them off the city walls to make more room, and who took their crops and their daughters and anything else that took their fancy. It was this cruel, insolent, rapacious city to which God sent Jonah.

But Jonah didn't want to go. His attitude was typical of the average Jew of the time. The average Jew was unconcerned about conditions in a heathen city, Ninevah or any other. He didn't care whether the people were happy, or even good. That wasn't his responsibility. So Jonah, although he heard the voice of God, did not choose to obey. He decided this would be a good time to take a trip, but instead of going east, toward Nineveh, he would go west. He would take a cruise on the Mediterranean. He thought, in accordance with the consensus of the time, that he could leave God in Palestine.

He went down to Joppa, on the coast, and found a ship ready to sail for Tarshish (an old name for Cadiz). Excellent! It was at the far end of the Mediterranean. He bought a ticket and went on board, found his cabin and went to sleep, feeling perfectly secure. It never occurred to him that God might outwit him. But he little knew the surprises in store for him.

I think right here the author began to smile as he prepared to reveal that Jehovah's power did not stop at the water's edge, that he is God even on the Mediterranean Sea. That night (he wrote)

God sent out a great wind that blew up such a storm that even the hardened sailors were frightened. They called frantically on their gods, while throwing overboard all unnecessary cargo to lighten the ship. But neither course did any good. They decided some god had a hand in this, so in order to find out who had been offended by whom, they cast lots. This required all hands on deck, so the captain went to get Jonah. He found the traveler asleep, which exasperated him. He exclaimed, "Man, how could you sleep through this? You had better be up praying to whatever gods you believe in. Anyway, we are going to draw lots to see who is responsible for this storm, so get up on deck."

They drew lots, and Jonah got the one marked guilty—not surprising, since God was running the lottery. That surprised the sailors, however. They knew they were rough sinful men, but apparently this smooth well-to-do passenger was even more sinful. They were curious about why and asked questions—who his god was, where he lived, what he had done wrong. When Jonah confessed that he had disobeyed his God, they couldn't under-stand. Murder or theft they could accept as sins, but why this god would stir up such a storm for such a small matter was beyond their comprehension. So they had to ask Jonah how to remedy the situation.

"Then what shall we do with you to appease him?"

"You'll have to throw me overboard," said our hero.

But this course was too inhumane for them. They refused. Instead, they went to the oars and rowed hard, but the storm grew worse. It looked as if it would either be Jonah or the whole crew, and Jonah kept nobly, but unrealistically, insisting they throw him over.

So, finally, they did. "And the sea ceased from her raging." Immediately a huge fish, which had been lolling around waiting for its cue, swam up and opened its mouth, and down went Jonah.

If this were history instead of fiction, Jonah's story would have ended right there. But the author (in my opinion) threw that episode in for pure comedy. I can easily imagine him chuckling over that quaint touch—his adapting Jeremiah's figure of speech to a supposedly real-life adventure.

(If he had known what a to-do this was going to cause for generations of literal-minded people, would he have restrained his sense of humor? . . . I doubt it.)

Another great strain put on the credulity of anyone determined to regard this story as fact is the inclusion of a poem, or hymn, composed by Jonah inside the whale, while seaweed was wrapped about his head (as he says himself) and his soul was fainting. It was a cry of repentance and a plea for forgiveness.

God had no intention of abandoning his disobedient servant to a fish, however, or to anything else. He wasn't through with him. Jonah had neither learned his lesson or performed his mission. So God had the fish get rid of him after three days, and he emerged on dry land none the worse for his rather unusual experience! He had learned one thing—that God is more powerful than he and just as stubborn—but his attitude toward the people of Ninevah had not changed. So it was in a vile humor that he set out for the city.

Ninevah was so large that it took three days to cross it. The author quaintly says that Jonah went a day's journey into it, and then on some plaza, or in the market place, perhaps, he began to preach. "Yet forty days and Ninevah shall be overthrown!" he cried. It was more of a tirade, full of angry references to their sins and threats of God's vengeance if they did not repent. Then another unlikely thing happened: they did repent! Everyone from the king down to the humblest person in the city! And God forgave and spared them.

If such a thing ever actually took place—if 100% of the population of a wicked city should be converted—it would be recorded in secular history, but in our story it is important only for the effect on Jonah, since the author's theme is the making of a missionary.

How would a real missionary, one you have met or heard speak, feel about such an event? He (or she) would be ecstatic, would he not? Overcome with delight that he had been a part of such a great conversion! Well, Jonah wasn't. He was angry. He declared indignantly that God had embarrassed him, had allowed him to go out on a limb and then chopped it off. He even said, sarcastically and untruthfully, that that was the reason he didn't want to go to Ninevah in the first place. "You plan to do evil," he raged at God, "and then you repent. I knew this would happen all the time. And now I'm so embarrassed I could die."

It is shocking to see Jonah thinking of himself, his comfort, his feelings, at a time like this. He's a complete egoist, thinking his silly feelings are important. I think all he cared about was going back home afterwards and bragging: "I was right about it, you know. I told them they were going to be destroyed, and they were. Right on the dot. Forty days to the minute." A very fundamental thing was wrong—he had no love for humanity. God's prophet was not like his God at all!

However, God was patient. He treated his reluctant servant like a spoiled child instead of a responsible adult. He said, "Jonah, aren't you ashamed to be angry?"

Jonah didn't answer. He went out of the city, climbed a hill, and sat down to sulk and wait to see what, if anything, was going to happen. There, he would be safe in case God should change his mind again and the city should be swallowed up by an earth-quake, leveled by a tornado, or consumed by flame. He was still hoping for the worst.

Now we have another ridiculous situation. The author makes a comedy of Jonah's fit of temperament and God's method of teaching him, while at the same time demonstrating tender care for his overwrought prophet. If God had been like many of us, he would have given up this man as a bad job, looked around for a better helper, and begun again. But Jonah, too, was important to God. He wanted to convert him as well as the Ninevites. So he planned a simple little object lesson, hoping to teach him the rudiments of religion. He did three things in rapid succession. He made a gourd vine grow up quickly to shade Jonah. And Jonah was pleased. But that night he sent a worm to eat it away near the root, and the vine died. And Jonah was grieved. Then to hasten his final lesson, God sent a vehement east wind and a hot sun, and Jonah had a touch of the latter and fainted.

When he came to, God said, "Jonah, aren't you ashamed to be angry on account of the gourd?"

"No, I'm not ashamed. I do well to be angry, even unto death," he said dramatically.

He was still selfishly wrapped up in himself, But there had been a feeling of pity for the dead gourd, as some people may pity animals, but not humans, and God built on that, for pity is akin to love.

So he said, "Jonah, you were sorry for the vine, which meant nothing to you. You had not planted, or watered, or tended it. If you will magnify that feeling many times, you can see how I would have felt about destroying Ninevah, a city of people, not gourd vines. People I created and have watched and tended hopefully. Men and women with souls, little helpless children, and babies so young they can't tell their right hands from their left."

That is the end. There is no hint as to whether Jonah was converted to God's view that all people are precious in his sight and became a willing missionary, or not.

Did the author suddenly dry up, run out of invention, have no notion how to end his tale?

I think he left it unfinished deliberately in order to suggest that he was writing about life, and only life could write the ending. For the fictional Jonah was not one man, but all Israel. The real-life Jonah, the son of Amittai, had been dead 500 years; his fate was irrelevant and immaterial. What did matter at this time was what the Israelites would do.

That nameless, understanding prophet, the author, was pleading with his generation, 200 years before the birth of Christ, to discard their narrow nationalistic prejudices and to carry the message of God's love to all the world.

There is a story of an old saint who lived centuries ago when religious people sometimes did very silly things. The story called him a saint. If he was indeed a saint, he was a very misguided one, or so it seems to me. He considered the world was so evil it ought to be destroyed, and he prayed to God to consume it with fire.

Fortunately for us, God does not grant all prayers. But this man, very hopeful and even expectant of having his granted, and wanting (I suspect) to get credit for being very pious and a power with God, announced to all and sundry that he was going to hold out his hand in protest against the wickedness of the world, and to keep it out until God had done what he asked, and made an end of it.

The days passed, and God took no action.

I suppose the "saint's" muscles adjusted; in those days they used to adjust to incredible things. As he stood there with his hand out, palm up, a little bird came and built a nest in it, laid some eggs and hatched her babies. Gradually, the man became interested. Then his protective instinct and tenderness were awakened, till the hand that was first stretched out in anger was kept extended in love.

It's the story of Jonah in medieval dress. Instead of a gourd vine, God used a little bird to break the hard crust of self-righteousness and to convince his servant that the religious life can never be built on contempt for people—that no one can love God who does not love his brothers also.

Conclusion

These brief profiles of a few of the people we encounter on that old, old trail that led out of Ur, show us that they *did* move, almost imperceptibly, upward, until they arrived at last at Bethlehem, where Isaiah's prophecy was finally fulfilled: "Unto us a child is born, unto us a Son is given."

It was truly said, "The past and future met in Jesus Christ."